Armour/Eide

Negotiating

Negotiating Brexit

by

John Armour

Horst Eidenmüller

2017

C. H. BECK · HART · NOMOS

Published by
Verlag C. H. Beck ohG, Wilhelmstraße 9, 80801 München, Germany,
eMail: bestellung@beck.de

Co-published by
Hart Publishing, Kemp House, Chawley Park, Cumnor Hill, Oxford, OX2 9PH, United
Kingdom, online at: www.hartpub.co.uk

and

Nomos Verlagsgesellschaft mbH & Co. KG Waldseestraße 3–5, 76530 Baden-Baden,
Germany, eMail: nomos@nomos.de

Published in North America (US and Canada) by Hart Publishing,
c/o International Specialized Book Services, 930 NE 58th Avenue, Suite 300,
Portland, OR 97213-3786, USA, eMail: orders@isbs.com

ISBN 978 3 406 71635 5 (C.H. BECK)
ISBN 978 1 50991 998 7 (HART)
ISBN 978 3 8487 4410 7 (NOMOS)

© 2017 Verlag C. H. Beck ohG
Wilhelmstr. 9, 80801 München
Printed in Germany by
Nomos Verlagsgesellschaft mbH & Co. KG
In den Lissen 12 D-76547 Sinzheim
Typeset by
Reemers Publishing Services GmbH, Krefeld
Cover: Druckerei C. H. Beck Nördlingen

Preface and Acknowledgements

Brexit is on its way: On 29 March 2017, the United Kingdom (UK) issued the withdrawal notice according to Article 50 of the Treaty on the Functioning of the European Union (TFEU), formally initiating the withdrawal process. *Negotiating Brexit* involves intricate legal, economic and political issues.

This volume brings together expert views on three key questions (for details see the Introduction): (i) Brexit Stakes: What is at stake with Brexit for crucial policy fields such as financial services, corporate activity, and legal (dispute resolution) services? (ii) Brexit Analytics: How is Brexit influenced by the negotiating framework of Article 50 TFEU, political constraints on the negotiations and the World Trade Organization (WTO) framework as an outside option? (iii) Brexit Process: Which negotiation strategies and process design/management are conducive for 'making Brexit a success' – or at least to avert a lose-lose outcome?

We hope that this volume is of interest to practitioners and policy-makers involved or interested in the legal, economic and political consequences of Brexit and to scholars researching Brexit Stakes, Brexit Analytics and/or Brexit Process.

We should like to thank all authors, who were working on a tight time-schedule, for their contributions. Special thanks for excellent support during the editorial process go to Clara Martins Pereira. We welcome the comments of readers on the issues raised in this volume. You can reach us at john.armour@law.ox.ac.uk and/or horst.eidenmueller@law.ox.ac.uk.

Oxford, July 2017

John Armour
Horst Eidenmüller

Table of Contents

Table of Contents

Table of Contents

Table of Contents

Introduction

John Armour and Horst Eidenmüller

Brexit is on its way. The formal withdrawal process under Article 50 Treaty on the Functioning of the European Union ('TFEU') was initiated on 29 March 2017. The United Kingdom ('UK') and the European Union ('EU') now have less than two years in which to negotiate the terms of the UK's withdrawal, and will seek at the same time to pursue a closely linked deal over the terms of their future relationship. By mid-2019, the UK will, it seems, have left the EU – unless the Brexit process is reversed politically.

Brexit will have fundamental political, economic and legal consequences – for Britain, Europe and, indeed, the world. These consequences will be shaped by the features of the agreement that is to be negotiated. These negotiations will be complex, involving multiple parties and issues. The UK government has indicated its desire to impose meaningful controls on immigration from the EU. And the EU has ruled out continued UK access to the single market without continued recognition of the four fundamental freedoms, including free movement. This seems to imply that a 'soft' Brexit, in which the UK remains a participant in the European Economic Area and the single market, is no longer possible.

Hence, at this point, possible configurations for the UK's future relationship with the EU appear to include: (i) 'Hard' Brexit: the UK leaves the single market and imposes controls on immigration from the EU. The terms of market access for goods and services have to be negotiated. Wide-ranging trade negotiations of this sort normally take many years to complete; (ii) 'Harder' Brexit: if no agreement is reached on the terms of the future relationship, then only the WTO framework will restrict the mutual imposition of tariffs; there will be no effective restrictions on non-tariff barriers, which are particularly prevalent as regards services;[1] and (iii) 'Hardest' Brexit: the Article 50 period comes to an end without any agreement having been reached regarding either the future relationship or even the terms of the UK's exit from the EU.

On 17 March 2017, we organised a workshop at St Hugh's College, Oxford, entitled 'Negotiating Brexit'. The day's discussions brought together leading academics, practitioners and policymakers who are involved in the ensuing Brexit negotiations. Their unifying perspective was how to realize the best (or least-worst) outcome in these negotiations. The discussions were divided into three sections: the first ('Brexit Stakes') was concerned with what is at stake,

---

[1] Some (limited) market access may be available in sectors, such as financial services, where the EU, at its discretion, may unilaterally recognise third country rules as 'equivalent'.

and in particular for the UK. The focus here was on crucial policy fields such as financial services, corporate activity, and legal (dispute resolution) services. In the second section ('Brexit Analytics'), the negotiating framework of Article 50 TFEU, political constraints on the negotiations and the World Trade Organisation ('WTO') framework as an outside option were analyzed. Finally, in a third section ('Brexit Process') negotiation specialists and mediators discussed negotiation strategies and process design/management for 'making Brexit a success' – or at least avert a lose-lose outcome.

Contributions to the conference were published in a special 'Brexit Negotiations Series' of the Oxford Business Law Blog[2] roughly in the order of the conference contributions, grouped together by conference themes. The first was a post based on a keynote delivered by Professor Clemens Fuest from the University of Munich/CESifo. For publication in this volume, the authors updated and revised their posts, adding references where deemed appropriate or necessary. However, the conversational character of the contributions as blog posts was in general retained.

> *John Armour is the Hogan Lovells Professor of Law and*
> *Finance at the University of Oxford.*
> *Horst Eidenmüller is the Freshfields Professor of*
> *Commercial Law at the University of Oxford.*

---

[2] See Horst Eidenmüller, 'Brexit Negotiations Series: Introduction' (*Oxford Business Law Blog*, 3 April 2017) <https://www.law.ox.ac.uk/business-law-blog/blog/2017/04/brexit-negotiations-series-introduction> accessed 5 June 2017.

Brexit: Economic Issues

Clemens Fuest

On 29 March 2017 the United Kingdom ('UK') government declared its intention to leave the European Union ('EU'). In the next two years, the EU 27 and the UK will negotiate the terms of Britain's exit and its future relations with the EU. It is possible to extend this deadline, but both sides have an interest in concluding the negotiations as soon as possible. At the same time, it is far from clear whether such negotiations will lead to an agreement. Without an agreement, EU membership of the UK will end in March 2019, and trade relations will fall back on World Trade Organisation ('WTO') rules. Of course, such a result would be a burden on future political and economic relations between the EU and the UK.

What are the most important economic issues in the Brexit negotiations? First and most importantly, the UK and the EU will need to agree on the regime for the trade of goods and services. Second, new rules are needed for migration. Third, the UK needs to be disentangled financially from the EU ('Brexit Bill').

1. Red lines

Both sides started the negotiations with 'red lines'. For the UK, there seem to be three red lines. The UK wants to have full control over immigration, and it does not want the rulings of the European Court of Justice to apply to the UK any longer. It also wants full sovereignty over its trade policy. On the EU side, one red line is that EU citizens currently living in the UK must retain their rights. Moreover, there is a lot of talk about the indivisible nature of the internal market's four basic freedoms, meaning, in particular, that the EU wants to respond to limits on migration by restricting trade in financial services. There are also frequent warnings that there is to be no cherry-picking, although it is unclear what that actually means. Any deal with the UK will be a bespoke agreement specially tailored to the particular conditions of Brexit. Finally, the view is widespread that the EU 27 cannot allow Brexit to be an economic success because that might encourage others to follow.

2. Future trade in goods and services

Given that the UK wants national sovereignty over its trade policy, European Internal Market membership and a customs union with common external tariffs are ruled out, so a free trade agreement for goods, and possibly also services, seems to be the only possible arrangement. Compared to no agreement, which would imply trade under WTO rules, a free trade agreement would make a big difference. A comprehensive agreement ensuring free trade in goods and services would preserve most of the benefits implied by the single market, even though some additional hurdles, like rules of origin, would also arise. According to estimates based on trade simulation models carried out by researchers at the ifo Institute[1], the losses caused by a switch to a regime with a comprehensive free trade agreement would be 0.4 per cent of GDP for the UK and 0.1 per cent for the EU. In the case of a 'hard Brexit', that means falling back on WTO rules, the estimated losses would amount to 1.7 per cent for the UK and 0.4 per cent for the EU. In absolute terms, the losses are of similar magnitude. One should note that these simulations focus on 'static losses', which result from the failure to use comparative advantages. These calculations fail to include dynamic losses resulting from reduced competition, which is likely to lead to reduced innovation. This implies that the GDP losses described above are only lower bound estimates of the true losses.

For business, the uncertainty surrounding Brexit is a problem that will grow as the exit date in 2019 approaches. At the moment, companies on both sides of the channel must face up to the prospect of tariffs applying as of 2019, or regulatory barriers arising that will endanger existing business models. If this risk cannot be dispelled, adjustments need to be made very quickly. The British economy is integrated into Europe-wide supply chains in a wide variety of ways and it would be costly for both sides to restructure these chains now, just to prepare for the possibility that the negotiations fail to result in an agreement. To avoid such costs, it is important to outline the shape of future economic relations as quickly as possible, as well as to define the transition phase starting in 2019 and where the existing rules for trade will continue to apply for a number of years to avoid disruption.

3. Migration

While there is no doubt that the UK wants full control over migration, the question of what that means in practice remains open. Protecting the existing rights of foreigners living in the UK will be a necessary condition for an agreement with the EU. Regarding future migration, it would be conceivable to provide for a kind of emergency brake to be activated in case of an excessively high wave of immigration, along similar lines to the Swiss arrangement. However, since limiting immigration played a central role in the Brexit referendum, that may not be enough from the UK perspective.

---

[1] Gabriel Felbermayr et al, 'Ökonomische Effekte eines Brexit auf die Deutsche und Europäische Wirtschaft' (2017) Studie des ifo Instituts im Auftrag des Bundesministeriums für Wirtschaft und Energie (BMWi) <https://www.cesifo-group.de/portal/pls/portal/!POR-TAL.wwpob_page.show?_docname=1604482.PDF> accessed 5 June 2017.

Economically, the gains from trade in goods and services are even higher when migration is restricted. However, politically achieving a deep free trade agreement will be more difficult, the more restrictive the UK wants to be on immigration.

4. The EU Budget and the 'Brexit Bill'

The last point is the 'Brexit Bill'. The European treaties do not include explicit rules and procedures to disentangle a Member State financially from the EU. There are two possible approaches.[2] The first is called the 'club membership' approach. It would imply that a country starts paying membership fees when it joins the EU and stops doing so on the day it leaves. No attempt is made to establish the assets and liabilities of the 'club' when a country joins or leaves. Under this approach, the UK would stop making contributions to the EU budget in 2019. The second is called the 'divorce approach'. According to this approach, the UK is responsible for its share of the EU's net liabilities and has to make a one off payment when it leaves. Unsurprisingly, the EU wants to apply the divorce approach. The European Commission has unofficially suggested a 'Brexit bill' of 60 billion euros. This bill covers various and partly contingent EU liabilities, including EU officials' pension claims and the '*reste à liquider*': that is, past spending commitments in the EU budget that have not yet been paid. Whether or not this *reste à liquider* is something the Member States actually owe is disputed. Several net contributors to the EU budget, including Germany, have argued that this is not the case. Overall, the determination of the Brexit bill is not an exercise in accounting, but a political negotiation. This is not necessarily bad news, because finding an overall agreement may require compensatory payments, and the Brexit bill negotiations offer enough room for achieving this.

5. Hard or Soft Brexit?

How likely is it that there will be a deal between the UK and the EU, and how constructive will that deal be? The British government has threatened to deny cooperation in security policy if the EU does not cooperate economically. This was received quite badly by the EU, with critics arguing that there should be no trade-off between security and economic benefits. At the same time, the Brexit coordinators of the European Parliament have announced that 'a State withdrawing from the Union cannot enjoy similar benefits as a European Union Member State and…therefore… [The European Parliament] will not consent to any agreement that would contradict this.'

An important factor for the negotiations is that there are considerable conflicts of interest between the EU 27 Member States. For instance, Ger-

---

[2] See Zsolt Darvas et al, 'Divorce Settlement or Leaving the Club? A Breakdown of the Brexit Bill' (2017) Bruegel Working Paper 03/2017 <http://bruegel.org/wp-content/uploads/2017/03/WP_2017_03-.pdf> accessed 5 June 2017.

many has a strong interest in maintaining free trade with the UK, whereas other Member States will place more emphasis on migration. Another key issue on the EU side is how to deal with the fact that there will be a gap in the EU budget when the net contributions of the UK disappear.[3] A possible deal among the EU 27 could include Germany paying more and getting free trade in goods and services with the UK. But whether the public debate on both sides, which is charged with emotions and resentment, allows for a rational compromise outcome remains an open question.

In the end, reaching an agreement capable of minimizing the economic costs of Brexit will require considerable energy, goodwill, and political skills on both sides.

Clemens Fuest is Professor of Economics at the
University of Munich and President of the Ifo Institute.

---

[3] Clemens Fuest and Daniel Stöhlker, 'Brexit: Budgetary Issues' (2017) Mimeo: ifo Institute.

Brexit Negotiations and their Impact on the Brexit Planning of Banks – As with Many Negotiation Processes, Timing is Everything

Johannes Adolff

Many European Union ('EU') banks are in the midst of their Brexit planning. Obviously, their micro level decisions are driven by what is happening in the Brexit negotiations on the macro level. Put more precisely, their decisions are driven by their current and cautious *predictions* of what will happen on the macro level. From the perspective of the governmental Brexit negotiation teams, this means that time is of the essence. If they wish to effectively create the 'right' incentives for banks, they must concentrate on signals with a *current* impact on predictions, rather than on eventual outcomes.

This observation can be broken down into three elements:

1. Observation 1: The two years are not two years

First, I argue that it would be wrong to assume that the two year negotiation period according to Art 50 TFEU is relevant for the Brexit planning of banks: the two years are not in fact two years. I submit that this observation holds true for both United Kingdom ('UK') banks currently active in the EU 27, and *vice versa*. For the sake of simplicity, I use one specific stylized set of facts:

Put yourselves in the shoes of the management of a US bank with a licensed UK subsidiary using EU passporting privileges to (a) do cross-border business out of the UK into certain continental EU 27 Member States and (b) having branches in other Member States – in the practitioner's lingo 'using the UK sub as the EU hub'. Currently, this means that only one EU banking license is needed, namely the one regarding the subsidiary located in the UK. With the UK government having served its notice under Art 50 TFEU in March 2017, this set-up remains stable until Q 1 of 2019.

Beyond that, there is uncertainty. The risk is that, post-Brexit, there will be no passporting, and no functional equivalent established as a result of the Brexit negotiations. Arguably, this risk is small. But, in the shoes of the board members in my example, having someone pointing out this low probability is not helpful. Rather, by taking into account the expected implementation period for their likely Brexit strategy – which should be carried out within the two year period set out in Art 50 para 3 TFEU – banks will come to the conclusion that their 'go/no-go'-decision must be taken at a rather earlier point in time. As a result, all that counts is their *prognosis horizon* at *that* point in time.

To the extent the outcome of the macro-level Brexit negotiations is still uncertain as of that 'go/no-go'-date, they might wish to err on the side of caution. In most jurisdictions, this is not only common sense, but is also the message of the law. Fundamentally endangering the sustainability of a company's business model is, as a rule, prohibited. If the magnitude of a risk is such that its realization would make it impossible – or, in this case, illegal in certain countries – to continue trading, then this risk must be avoided, even if the probability is low. Therefore, facing uncertainty, the banks' management teams will need to assume a very hard Brexit, ie no passporting post-Brexit, and no useful functional equivalent.

2. Observation 2: The critical window is no more than six months

In this scenario, the management in my example is left with four options. These are, radically simplified, the following:

(1) **Wind-down:** They can discontinue, as of March 2019, all EU 27 activities locally requiring a banking license.

(2) **Equivalence Application:** They can apply for recognition under an equivalence regime. For core banking activities, such as lending and taking deposits, there is no such regime at the EU level. Consequently, such an application will need to be filed with each national regulatory authority for each of the EU 27 Member States in question. If granted, it can become a basis for soliciting institutional customers cross-border. However, it will not be sufficient for retail, or for putting people permanently on the ground. Also, of course, there is always the risk that it may be unilaterally withdrawn, if and when the respective national regulator is not (any more) satisfied that the UK regulatory system remains 'equivalent' to its own.[1]

(3) **Branch:** Alternatively, management can apply for a national branch license. In most Member States, this process is similar to applying for a full banking license (and it has the disadvantage that a branch does not allow passporting). Thus, managers might as well go straight for a:[2]

(4) **Subsidiary** with a full banking license, which will then be their new EU hub, functionally replacing the one previously located in the UK.[3]

---

[1] Directorate General for Internal Policies – Economic Governance Support Unit, 'Briefing: Third-country equivalence in EU banking legislation' (*European Parliament,* 7 March 2017) <http://www.europarl.europa.eu/RegData/etudes/BRIE/2016/587369/IPOL_BRI(2016)587369_EN.pdf> accessed 31 May 2017.

[2] Wolf-Georg Ringe, 'The Irrelevance of Brexit for the European Financial Market' (2017) Legal Research Paper Series 10/2017, 9 <https://ssrn.com/abstract=2902715> accessed 31 May 2017.

[3] This may be revised and may require the establishment of an intermediate parent undertaking according to Art 21 b of the European Commission's Proposal for amending Directive 2013/36/EU (see European Commission, 'Proposal for a Directive of the European Parliament and of the Council amending Directive 2013/36/EU as regards exempted entities, financial holding companies, mixed financial holding companies, remuneration, supervisory measures and powers and capital conservation measures' COM (2016) 854 final).

Establishing branches and/or a subsidiary will take 12 to 18 months, the latter involving not only the local regulator, but also the European Central Bank ('ECB'). For both you need local substance. Often, you will thus need to move banking assets (and liabilities) across borders. Many of the tools for doing so, such as a cross-border merger, are currently available under EU law.[4] However, being cautious means assuming that such EU-tools will disappear in a hard Brexit scenario. Thus, to the extent you wish to use any such tools, your cross-border move needs to be fully completed pre-Brexit.[5]

3. Observation 3: Consequently, this issue cannot wait

For these reasons, any signals from the Brexit negotiation table capable of having a material impact on the Brexit planning of the banks need to (i) come very soon and to (ii) be close to 100 % reliable.

A 'nothing is agreed until everything is agreed' attitude will not entail the desired effect (in my example, of keeping high levels of banking substance in the UK).

A preferable approach may be to agree, at the beginning of the Art 50 period, on a 'grandfathering period'.[6] Such period could last, for example, 30 months from the conclusion of the negotiations or the end of the two year-period (plus extension, if any) under Art 50 TFEU, whichever occurs first. During this period, the current passporting system would continue to apply, to be automatically replaced by the end of this period with whatever will be agreed as the permanent solution in the Brexit negotiations.[7] On this basis, banks could wait for the eventual outcome and base their decision-making on their certain knowledge of such outcome, rather than on their uncertain current predictions.

Johannes Adolff is Partner at Hengeler Mueller
and a Professor at the Goethe University of Frankfurt.

---

[4] Council Directive 2005/56/EC of 26 October 2005 on cross-border mergers of limited liability companies [2005] OJ L 310/1.

[5] John Armour, Holger Fleischer, Vanessa Knapp and Martin Winner, 'Brexit and Corporate Citizenship' (2017) ECGI Working Paper Series in Law No 340/2017, 21, 30 <https://papers.ssrn.com/sol3/papers.cfm?abstract_id=2897419> accessed 31 May 2017.

[6] Ringe (n2).

[7] A member of the Executive Board of the European Central Bank suggested a transitional period for the approval or rejection of internal risk management models to establish an equivalent assessment instead of the passporting system (see Sabine Lautenschläger, 'Board Meeting' (AFME Board Meeting, Frankfurt, 22 March 2017) <https://www.ecb.europa.eu/press/key/date/2017/html/sp170322.en.html> accessed 31 May 2017).

Leaving the EU: Impact on Bank Customers

Luis Correia da Silva

For a long time, trading internationally used to be the reserve of large multinational corporations. However, the digital revolution implies that Small and Medium Enterprises ('SMEs') are now 'born' operating across borders and expect to be able to access international markets both for their inputs and to sell their products and services.

With the majority of firms' international payments going through a bank, banks have become critical pieces of infrastructure that allow firms to grow through the benefits of international trade.

Given this vital role for banks in international trade, it is important to understand what leaving the European Union ('EU') by the United Kingdom ('UK') means for the commercial banking sector. This short article examines what is at stake for banks in the case of Brexit, and the effect of Brexit on their employees, investors and, crucially, their customers. It is this last mechanism – the effect on customers – which can mean that small changes in banking can have wider impacts on the rest of the economy.

1. UK banks have a lot at stake

In 2016, UK banks generated around 25 % (£25bn) of their total revenues from clients and products linked to the EU (see Figure 1).[1] The pending exit of the UK from the EU is likely to trigger the relocation of some of this activity to other financial centres in the EU and elsewhere.

While widespread relocation is unlikely until the form of the post-exit arrangements becomes clearer, the uncertainty created in the interim is likely to dampen any plans among international banking groups to expand their UK-based operations.

---

[1] Oliver Wyman, 'Report: The Impact of the UK's Exit from the EU on the UK-based Financial Services Sector' (*TheCityUK*, 2016) <http://www.oliverwyman.com/content/dam/oliver-wyman/global/en/2016/oct/Brexit_POV.PDF> accessed 31 May 2017. This includes UK subsidiaries of international banking groups.

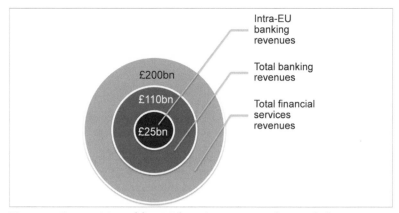

Figure 1: Composition of financial services revenues (2015, £bn)

Source: Oliver Wyman, 'The impact of the UK's exit from the EU on the UK-based financial services sector' (Report produced for TheCityUK, 2016).

2. Does it matter for staff and investors if banks relocate?

Current employees may find that their UK-based role becomes redundant and they have to seek alternative employment within the UK or apply for new roles created in places such as Frankfurt, Paris, or Dublin. Prospective employees may find that the scope for pursuing a banking career in the UK is curtailed. Overall, levels of employment in the UK banking sector are likely to be lower than would otherwise be the case. This effect will also ripple out beyond the banking sector to a range of closely related legal and professional services sectors that supply the banking sector.

Over the long run, some of the lower employment in banking could be expected to be offset by higher employment elsewhere in the economy as workers transition to other sectors, albeit at slightly lower wages. However, the adjustment could take several years and lead to a loss of productivity. Employment in the banking sector is also likely to settle at a permanently lower level due to lower net immigration of financial services professionals. This could have an impact on government revenues from sources such as income tax, national insurance, VAT, and stamp duty as less highly skilled international professionals are attracted to work in the UK banking sector.

The impact on bank investors will vary according to the type of activity banks undertake. Banks that serve clients in multiple EU countries from a UK base could be expected to adjust their organisational structures so that their access to markets is maintained. Some banks will be better positioned to make these adjustments (eg, where they already have a subsidiary in Europe); others will be at a relative disadvantage and face losing market share. This adjustment process will be risky for banks, requiring skilled management to navigate the transition successfully.

There will be costs associated with this transition to new structures, and probably higher costs in the new 'steady state' as a result of a less efficient model for delivering banking services than is currently the case. However, as most banks will be facing similar cost shocks, a large proportion of the additional costs are likely to be passed on to customers, rather than having a long-term impact on profitability. The impact on customers has received relatively little attention to date.

3. What about the users of banking services?

So who are the users of banking services? One way to think about this is to look at the different sources of bank revenues. Figure 2 shows the split between commercial, wholesale and retail users, for three large banks. All of these users could be affected by Brexit in different ways. Some areas that have received the least attention are the commercial customers, the corporates using banks for lending, cash management, payments and, importantly, cross-border transactions.

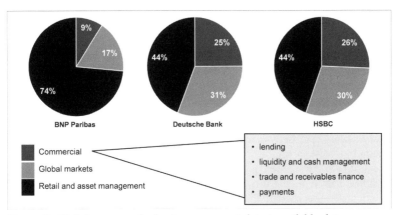

Figure 2: Global revenues by business segment, latest available data

Source: BNP Paribas, Deutsche Bank and HSBC company accounts.

4. Massive cross-border transactions between UK and EU businesses

When the impact of Brexit on commercial cross-border transactions is considered, the focus is usually on trade. The total amount of trade between the UK and other EU Member States is certainly large, at around £520 billion in 2015, but this is not the full picture. The links between the UK and other EU Member States run deeper than this, with cross-ownership of companies totalling some £1 trillion in 2015 (see Figure 3), and a broadly balanced split of ownership between the UK and other European countries/other EU Member States.

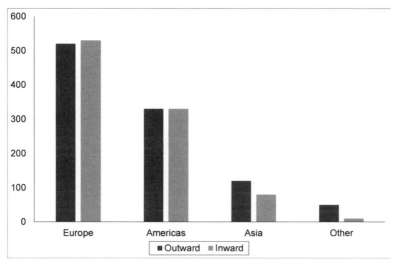

Figure 3: The value of subsidiaries and branches in EU/UK owned by UK/EU companies

Source: ONS (2015), 'Foreign direct investment involving companies'.

Based on the official statistics of revenues and net corporate worth in the UK National Accounts,[2] the subsidiaries represented in Figure 3 are likely to have revenues totalling around £250 billion *per annum*, which provides an indication of the amount of intra-company cross-border transactions taking place. This would come on top of the transactions required for the £520 billion of trade each year.

The scale of the cross-border transactions being conducted suggests that even a small increase in transaction costs could produce a significant cost for the users of banking services, just as a small financial transaction tax can create significant costs in the financial system.[3] The exit of the UK from the EU could affect the cost of these cross-border transactions for a number of reasons. In the first few years, while the overall regulatory regime is likely to be similar, there could be increased costs due to the loss of EU 'passporting rights' for banks. These rights allow banks to provide a wide range of banking services for their clients operating between the UK and the rest of Europe. This means that companies can conduct intra-EU transactions through a

---

[2] Office for National Statistics, 'UK National Accounts, The Blue Book: 2016' (29 July 2016) <https://www.ons.gov.uk/economy/grossdomesticproductgdp/compendium/united-kingdomnationalaccountsthebluebook/2016edition> accessed 31 May 2017. See also Office for National Statistics, 'UK input-output analytical tables' (9 March 2016) <https://www.ons.gov.uk/economy/nationalaccounts/supplyandusetables/datasets/ukinputoutputanalyticaltablesdetailed> accessed 31 May 2017.

[3] Oxera explored the implications of a proposed EU financial transactions tax in Oxera, 'What could be the economic impact of the proposed financial transaction tax?' (2014) <http://www.oxera.com/Latest-Thinking/Publications/Reports/2014/What-could-be-the-economic-impact-of-the-proposed.aspx> accessed 31 May 2017.

single bank, giving customers access to economies of scale and scope. These passporting rights are likely to be lost, and, for many users of banking services (especially in the UK), this is likely to result in the duplication of transaction costs.

In the longer term, financial regulation may begin to diverge more fundamentally, potentially also affecting transaction costs. The UK has tended to lead financial regulation in many areas in Europe, but this leadership role is likely to change once outside of the EU – significant differences in approach could arise. Needing to comply with different regulatory regimes creates additional costs for banks, which are likely to be passed on to end-users. On the other hand, the new regulatory regime could reduce transaction costs if it were more efficient, but achieving such an improvement is quite uncertain.

In the long run, more fundamental shifts in the location of banks could have implications for end-users. If the UK's departure from the EU results in some non-UK wholesale banks leaving London, their commercial arms are also likely to exit, lessening choice and competition in the UK. New commercial banking institutions would also be less likely to enter the UK if the transaction costs rose and UK-based banks no longer had passporting rights. These effects could weaken competition and reduce innovation in banking services.

5. Will the UK leaving the EU affect end-users?

It is difficult at this stage to predict what could be the impact of leaving the EU on transaction costs and, hence, the end-users of banking services. The impact depends on the outcome of the negotiations and on how the banking sector itself responds to the changes. What is clear, however, is that the potential impact is significant simply because of the sheer number of transactions being conducted across borders, relying on the efficiency of the banking system. People and companies using banking services should not be forgotten in the Brexit negotiations.

Luis Correia da Silva is partner at
Oxera Consulting LLP.

The Landscape for Post-Brexit European Financial Services

Thierry Philipponnat

Brexit will be anything but negligible for the organisation of European finance.

Financial services firms based in the United Kingdom ('UK') generate today *circa* £150 bn *per annum* of revenues and, if ancillary services are included, £225 bn. These numbers represent, respectively, 8 % and 12 % of British Gross Domestic Product ('GDP'). It is estimated that up to 20 % of the revenues of the City of London are related to services sold into the European Union ('EU') single market; therefore, such revenues stand to be impacted by Brexit. It should further be noted that the City of London is also a major contributor to the UK Government budget with £71.4bn of tax receipts (11.5 % of total receipts) for HM Treasury in 2016.[1]

This short article looks at three issues related to the functioning of post-Brexit European financial services:

1. What legal regime will prevail tomorrow for City of London firms to service the EU 27 single market?

City of London firms selling services into the EU single market have relied so far on the so-called 'European financial passport'. A 'European financial passport' is an authorisation granted by the financial regulator of a Member State that is valid throughout the Union. Financial passports are granted at a very granular level: according to the Financial Conduct Authority ('FCA'), 5,500 City-based firms rely today on 336,421 passports to conduct business in the European Union.

By definition, an authorisation granted by a UK financial authority after Brexit will not be an authorisation granted by a Member State regulator. Financial activities authorised only by the British regulator will lose their passport to access the EU single market from the day Brexit comes into effect.

In theory, a so-called 'third country equivalence regime' could also give UK regulated firms access to the EU market. However, EU 27 authorities have always intended this regime to be a tool to open the EU market for incremental (and relatively marginal) business from third countries – and

---

[1] City of London, 'City of London Corporation Research Report: Total Tax Contribution of UK Financial Services – Ninth Edition' (2006) <https://www.cityoflondon.gov.uk/business/economic-research-and-information/research-publications/Documents/research%202016/total-tax-report-2016.pdf> accessed 6 June 2017.

not the main mechanism to regulate financial activity. It must also be noted that if the UK wanted to benefit from the EU equivalence regime in the future, it would need to follow the evolutions of European financial regulation and become a European regulation taker, when it used to be a regulation maker. Given the current momentum of British political life, this does not seem to be a likely scenario.

All in all, the future substance of the third country equivalence regime is unpredictable, and it would be highly risky for a City firm to count on it to develop its EU business after Brexit.

This leaves City of London firms conducting business in the EU with only one choice: relocating operations requiring a passport to the EU. But, interestingly, a debate is now growing between EU regulators about the substance to be required from City firms to grant them an authorisation to move in. The debate promises to be fierce, and its outcome will be a key factor to determine the materiality of the operations actually relocated from London to the various EU 27 financial centres competing to attract business.

2. Will the European economy be able to access the financial services it needs without London after Brexit?

Different categories of services must be considered:

a) Capital markets funding services

Capital markets funding services are based on the ability of issuers to access the pools of investors they need via investment banking teams analysing, selling, and trading their securities. Given the fact that there is no such thing as a 'London financial market,' a 'Paris financial market,' or a 'Frankfurt financial market,' but rather different global markets for different financial products, the fact that investment banking teams relocate from London to an EU 27 financial centre will have no impact on their ability to service investors and issuers and, therefore, on market liquidity, or on the cost of funding of issuers. However, according to AFME, 'the analysis of capital raising activity suggests that around two-thirds of debt and equity capital raised by EU corporates (is) facilitated by banks based in the UK (both UK headquartered and non-UK headquartered)'.[2] This means that City firms face a significant challenge to reorganise their operations to be able to service their clients after Brexit. But this reorganisation challenge concerns investment banks, not issuers or investors, and it will have a very limited impact for the latter.

---

[2] Association for Financial Markets in Europe – PWC, 'Planning for Brexit: Operational Impacts on Wholesale Banking and Capital Markets in Europe' (January 2017) <https://www.afme.eu/globalassets/downloads/publications/afme-pwc-planning-for-brexit.pdf> accessed 6 June 2017.

b) Hedging services

Hedging services are about derivatives trading, which is an oligopoly between a dozen of the largest banks of the world. Four EU banks play an essential role in the small world of large derivatives players, and those banks will continue to service their customers from their home countries after Brexit. It can also be expected that their American, Swiss or British competitors will choose to relocate to cities based in EU 27 Member States. Provision of hedging services to the European economy after Brexit will therefore not be an issue, notwithstanding the question of the continuity of existing contracts that needs to be addressed carefully.

c) Commercial banking, insurance, and asset management services

The description of the respective regimes and issues at stake in commercial banking, insurance, and asset management services is beyond the scope of this contribution, but the common denominator between those activities is that the impact of Brexit will be felt by the professionals involved, whilst having limited consequences for customers. This is due to existing competition and sometimes relatively low levels of UK-EU 27 business taking place. For instance, the direct provision of loans by UK-domiciled banks to Euro area non-financial firms at the end of 2016 stood at 1 % (€ 67bn) of total loans extended.[3] In asset management, even if the distribution of UK products to the EU market will be impacted, in particular in that relating to so-called 'UCITS' (Undertakings for Collective Investments in Transferable Securities), it is unlikely that Brexit will have a significant impact on customers, given the intense competition and plethora of alternative solutions.

3. Clearing of euro-denominated financial products: the biggest unknown of the landscape for post-Brexit European financial services

Up to 70 % of the clearing of Euro-denominated derivatives transactions take place today in London. The dominant player is LCH Ltd, with over € 500bn daily clearing activity of euro-denominated products[4] by SwapClear.

The dilemma for European regulators on clearing is how to strike the right balance between the principle of free competition at the heart of the financial system and their responsibility to ensure financial stability. Free competition is a strong reason for the clearing of euro-denominated derivatives products to continue to take place in London (private actors have no interest in

---

[3] European Central Bank, 'Financial Stability Review' (May 2017) <https://www.ecb.europa.eu/pub/pdf/other/ecb.financialstabilityreview201705.en.pdf?60c526239a8ecb2b6a81c-fedd898cc0d> accessed 6 June 2017.

[4] Source: LCH Group <www.lch.com> accessed 24 May 2017.

changing the *status quo*), whilst financial stability pushes European regulators to want to see the activity relocated to the Eurozone, so that they can regulate and supervise it.

This is a typical moral hazard situation: if the clearing of euro-denominated derivatives products remains in London, the profits from the activity will benefit London, but any losses that arise from an accident will be borne by the European Central Bank and, potentially, by the EU Member States' taxpayers. Knowing that the total notional amount of outstanding euro-denominated derivatives products cleared by SwapClear (LCH Group) stands at € 87 trillion,[5] over 8 times the size of the Eurozone GDP, it seems that the European authorities have a point: the failure of the LCH Group could have disastrous consequences for the financial stability of the Eurozone and its monetary policy. It can also be understood that the European authorities consider it to be their responsibility to supervise the clearing of an amount of euro-denominated activity of obvious systemic nature.

The stage for the debate on clearing services is set: the City of London and British authorities will plead for the *status quo* on the ground of free competition and lost cross-margining benefits for customers if the clearing of euro-denominated products is to be split from the clearing of products denominated in other currencies. Conversely, European authorities will plead to repatriate the clearing of euro-denominated financial products into the EU 27 on the ground of their duty to ensure the financial stability of the Eurozone and their unwillingness to be on the wrong side of the moral hazard balance.

To this day, this is the biggest unknown of the coming Brexit financial services negotiations and 'rapport de force'.

As a general conclusion, it is argued that London will remain without doubt Europe's main financial centre post-Brexit, but the previous trend towards the concentration of the European financial industry in a single centre will be reversed. The extent of this phenomenon will depend on the outcome of the debate between European regulators on the substance they should require from City firms in exchange for a financial passport and on the result of the debate on clearing services. In any case, Brexit will not have a significant impact on the ability of the European economy to access the financial services it needs, or on the cost of funding for European corporates and households.

Thierry Philipponnat is
the Director of the Institut Friedland.

---

[5] At the close of business on May 24 2017, the amount of outstanding euro-denominated derivatives products cleared by SwapClear stood at € 87,289,942,024,364 according to the LCH Group (see LCH Group, 'Daily Volumes' (2017) <http://www.lch.com/asset-classes/otc-interest-rate-derivatives/volumes> accessed 24 May 2017).

Brexit and Financial Services:
Bargaining in the Shadow of Equivalence*

John Armour

1. Financial services in the UK and the EU

'Financial services' comprise all the activities undertaken in the financial system – the sector that channels savings from consumers toward firms and households that need finance for investment or current consumption. It includes banks, asset managers, financial markets, and insurance. Financial services are a very important sector of the United Kingdom's ('UK's') economy, accounting for 7–12 % of Gross Domestic Product ('GDP'), 11 % of gross tax receipts, and 7–12 % of employment.[1] Financial services also provide the largest trade surplus for any sector of the UK economy, valued at £72 bn in 2014, of which £19 bn is with the rest of the European Union ('EU').[2]

Table 1: EU component of UK financial services revenue, by sector (2015, £ bn)

Sector	Banking	Asset management	Insurance	Market infrastructure	Total
Intra-EU revenues	27	6	5	12	50
Total revenues	117	23	42	26	208
EU fraction of total sector revenues	0.23	0.26	0.12	0.46	0.24
Sector fraction of total EU revenues	0.54	0.12	0.10	0.24	1.00

---

* This chapter is a substantially modified version of 'Brexit and Financial Services' (2017) 33 *Oxford Review of Economic Policy* S54-S69, available at https://academic.oup.com/oxrep/issue/33/suppl_1, and is reprinted with permission.

[1] Although it is common to think of this as an issue for 'the City', two-thirds of these employees are based outside London (see House of Lords EU Committee, 'Brexit: Financial Services' (2016) 9th Report of Session 2016–17 HL Paper 81, 5; Oliver Wyman, 'The Impact of the UK's Exit from the EU on the UK-Based Financial Services Sector' (2016) Report Commissioned for TheCityUK <http://www.oliverwyman.com/content/dam/oliver-wyman/global/en/2016/oct/Brexit_POV.PDF> accessed 8 June 2017.

[2] Data from TheCityUK.

Notes: Revenue data are from a study conducted by Oliver Wyman (see Oliver Wyman (n1) 6). 'Intra-EU revenues' comprise UK financial services revenues from international and wholesale business related to the EU; 'Banking' includes investment banking; 'Insurance' includes reinsurance; 'Market infrastructure' includes other financial services.

Table 1 reports UK revenues for different types of financial service during 2015, and the component of these generated by intra-EU international business. As can be seen, banking is by far the largest sector overall and accounts for 54 % of intra-EU financial services revenue. However, it is notable that a smaller proportion of the UK's total banking revenues are intra-EU (23 %) than for market infrastructure (46 %) or even asset management (26 %).

Sectoral differences also matter from the perspective of the EU, as Figure 1 illustrates. This shows the proportion of total EU28 activity of various types taking place in the UK. As a baseline, the UK accounts for 17 % of the entire EU GDP. This is closely tracked by the fraction of EU bank assets held by UK banks (21 per cent). However, the UK's share of total EU activity grows as we move to the right of Figure 1, encompassing equity market capitalization (30 %), numbers of globally systemically important banks (31 %), and especially wholesale market activities. Table 1 and Figure 1 together suggest that while banking is the largest component of the UK's intra-EU financial services revenues, the UK's greatest intra-EU comparative advantage lies in asset management and wholesale markets.

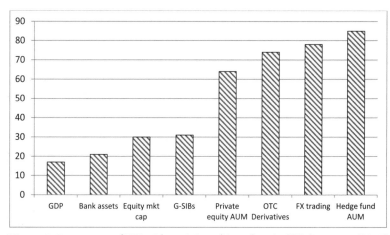

Figure 1: Percentage of EU-wide activity taking place in UK, by sector (2015)

Notes: GDP and equity market data are from the World Bank. Bank asset data are from the European Central Bank ('ECB') and the Prudential Regulation Authority ('PRA'). Data on G-SIBs (global systemically important banks) are from the Financial Stability Board ('FSB'). Data on private equity assets under management ('AUM'), over-the-counter ('OTC') derivatives transactions, foreign exchange ('FX') trading, and hedge fund AUM are from TheCityUK.

The outsize representation of the UK in the EU's financial market activity reflects the traditionally more market-oriented focus of the UK's domestic financial system than those of its continental European neighbours.[3] Conversely, financial market activity is under-represented in the rest of the EU, as reflected in the EU's assessment of its priorities for the financial sector. In 2015, the European Commission announced an ambitious programme of reform known as the Capital Markets Union ('CMU'), intended to spur the growth of capital markets throughout the EU.[4] This is motivated by concern that the EU's financial system is excessively dependent on banks, which is thought to have an adverse impact on the financing of innovation, and to render the system very dependent on the stability of large financial institutions.[5]

Thus, the financial services nexus between the UK and the rest of the EU is of strategic importance to both sides. It is a particularly successful UK export industry, and – at least as regards wholesale markets – also vitally important for the EU's diversification away from reliance on banking.

2. Financial services and EU law

The financial sector is one of the most globally interconnected components of most economies. It is at the same time one of the most heavily regulated sectors, the intensity of which has further heightened since the financial crisis.[6] The legal starting point, however, is that firms engaged in international activity must comply with regulation separately in each country in which they operate. There is a wide carve-out under the World Trade Organization ('WTO') rules that gives governments power to restrict cross-border financial services on the basis of prudential controls.[7] This consequently increases the cost of cross-border capital flows, with firms often

---

[3] See Wendy Carlin and Colin Mayer, 'Finance, Investment, and Growth' (2003) J Financ Econ 69, 191–226; Raghuram Rajan and Luigi Zingales, 'Banks and Markets: The Changing Character of European Finance' in Vítor Gaspar, Philipp Hartmann, and Olaf Sleijpen (eds) *The Transformation of the European Financial System* (Frankfurt, European Central Bank 2003) 123–68.

[4] European Commission, 'Green Paper: Building a Capital Markets Union' COM (2015) 63 final.

[5] European Systemic Risk Board, 'Is Europe Over-Banked?' (2014) Advisory Scientific Committee Report No 4 <https://www.esrb.europa.eu/pub/pdf/asc/Reports_ASC_4_1406.pdf> accessed 8 June 2017; Sam Langfield and Marco Pagano, 'Bank Bias in Europe: Effects on Systemic Risk and Growth' (2015) ECB Working Paper No 1797 <https://www.ecb.europa.eu/pub/pdf/scpwps/ecbwp1797.en.pdf?21971652ba3f7c1925aaadb3b5a5ae2> accessed 8 June 2017.

[6] John Armour, Dan Awrey, Paul Davies, Luca Enriques, Jeffrey N Gordon, Colin Mayer and Jennifer Payne, *Principles of Financial Regulation* (OUP 2016).

[7] World Trade Organisation, 'General Agreement on Trade in Services', Annex on Financial Services, para 2(a) < https://www.wto.org/english/tratop_e/serv_e/10-anfin_e.htm> accessed 8 June 2017.

needing to incorporate a subsidiary in each of the other jurisdictions in which they wish to operate, to ensure that each entity is compliant with the local regulatory regime.

A very different legal regime operates within the EU. The member states have agreed to a common corpus of financial regulation, which since the financial crisis is written through EU-level sectoral agencies.[8] In return, financial services firms that obtain authorization within this single rule-book from the national competent authority ('NCA') in their country are then free to offer services throughout the EU member states without any need for further local authorizations. This is known as the 'financial services passport'. Technically, there are many separate passports available under different pieces of financial services legislation, but they operate in an additive way, and EU law encompasses so much of financial services, that from most firms' perspective, the consequence is simply that whatever they are locally authorized to do, they are authorized to do throughout the EU. The loss of this ability to 'passport' services throughout the EU is at the centre of the financial sector's concerns over Brexit.

3. Brexit bargaining over financial services

Versions of Brexit in which the UK leaves the EU but remains a member of the European Economic Area ('EEA'), hence enjoying continued access to the single market and permitting UK-authorized financial services firms to keep their passporting rights under EU regulation, appear now to be politically unlikely. This is because EEA membership entails acceptance of the 'four freedoms' including continued free movement of persons, which has been ruled out by the UK Government. Nevertheless, given the level of UK–EU activity described above, there are clear benefits to both sides in coming to some sort of bilateral agreement regarding financial services.[9]

The existing precedents for bilateral agreements with the EU do not look promising. Switzerland and the EU have agreed a wide-ranging bundle of bilateral measures.[10] These cover free trade in goods, but generally not services, although there are particular measures on certain financial services, including non-life insurance.[11] However, the price for these agreements is that the EU requires Switzerland to accept the free movement of EU citizens,

---

[8] See Marco Lamandini and David Ramos Muñoz, *EU Financial Law: An Introduction* (Milan, Wolters Kluwer 2016); Niamh Moloney, 'The Impact of the EU Exit on Financial Services' (House of Commons Economy Committee, 11 October 2016).

[9] Wolf-Georg Ringe, 'The Irrelevance of Brexit for the European Financial Market' (2017) Oxford Legal Studies Research Paper No 10/2017 <https://papers.ssrn.com/sol3/papers.cfm?abstract_id=2902715> accessed 8 June 2017.

[10] Swiss Federal Department of Foreign Affairs, 'The Major Bilateral Agreements Switzerland–EU' (2016) <https://www.eda.admin.ch/content/dam/dea/en/documents/folien/Folien-Abkommen_en.pdf> accessed 8 June 2017.

[11] Stefan Hoffmann, 'Evidence on "Brexit and Financial Services"' to House of Lords Select Committee on the European Union Financial Affairs Sub-Committee (12 October 2016).

which would be problematic as a matter of UK politics. In contrast, the recently negotiated Comprehensive Economic and Trade Agreement ('CETA') between Canada and the EU does not entail any commitment on Canada's part to free movement of persons, but its provisions on financial services do not extend anywhere near the 'passport' recognition enjoyed by firms authorized within the EU (see CETA, ch 13). Moreover, CETA took 7 years to negotiate, and notoriously nearly failed to be ratified by EU member states.

However, the UK's bargaining position is quite unlike that of Switzerland or Canada, so these precedents are not especially illuminating. It is perhaps more helpful to consider the impact on financial services if no such agreement is reached. This will help to identify what is at stake if agreement is not reached, and the strength of the parties' bargaining positions.

4. The outside option: Third country equivalence

The cessation of EU/EEA membership will mean that the UK immediately becomes a 'third country'. The starting point is that financial services firms from third countries must obtain authorization for branches under the regulatory regimes of each member state in which they wish to operate: a decentralized model of state-by-state authorization,[12] very much like before the EU existed. EU law only intrudes in a negative way: most EU financial services legislation contains provisions prohibiting member states from offering more favourable treatment to third-country firms than is provided for under the EU regime for member state firms. Thus, the EU law rules provide a floor for third-country firms' compliance obligations, preventing any member state from offering a lax 'back door' to the single market. Yet, there is nothing to stop member states from discriminating *against* third-country firms by imposing more exacting standards than for EU firms.[13]

The most obvious way to avoid the foregoing difficulties is for third country firms to set up subsidiaries in the EU, which will then of course *be* EU firms. Unfortunately for the UK, this is – or was – the rationale for many foreign

---

[12] One apparent exception is the right to free movement of capital, which the EU Treaty expressly extends to movements between member states and third countries: Treaty on the Functioning of the European Union ('TFEU'), Art 63. However, this provides no real benefit to third-country financial services firms, because the provision has been interpreted narrowly by the Court of Justice such that where it overlaps with other treaty freedoms—such as the freedom of establishment—that do not extend to third countries, precedence should be given to the narrower provision (see Wolfgang Schön, 'Free Movement of Capital and Freedom of Establishment' (2016) 17 EBOR 229–260). Consequently, financial services firms cannot rely on the free movement of capital to conduct business in the EU, as this activity is covered by the freedom of establishment, which does not extend to third-country firms: Case C-452/04, *Fidium Finanz AG v Bundesanstalt für Finanzdienstleistungsaufsicht* [2006] ECR I-09521, ECLI:EU:C:2006:631.

[13] One area in which such discrimination might plausibly occur is in relation to the clearing of Euro-denominated derivatives contracts.

firms basing subsidiaries in London. The future of such UK subsidiaries may be called into doubt by loss of their passporting entitlements.

This rather unpromising regulatory terrain has been reshaped quite considerably, however, since the financial crisis. This period has seen a ramping-up in both the scope and intensity of international norms in financial regulation.[14] There has also been a shift in emphasis in financial regulation toward financial stability.[15] Because the preservation of financial stability necessitates international cooperation, and because differential regulation increases the costs of trade under a traditional decentralized authorization framework, there has been a parallel shift to multilateral production of new standards, through a new international organization established by the G20, the Financial Stability Board ('FSB'). As a by-product, firms in third countries compliant with FSB guidance are now subject to rules that are substantially similar to those in the EU.

These developments have also given the EU reason to rethink its traditional decentralized authorization model for third-country firms. Increasing the level of required scrutiny brings increased costs for each national authorization, and decentralized decision-making makes it harder to control systemic risk.[16] The result has been an emerging, and still-evolving, body of rules known loosely as 'third-country equivalence' (or '3CE') provisions.[17] In essence, these provide for centralized authorization decisions for third-country firms as regards certain aspects of the EU's financial regulation regime. Relevant third-country firms are thereby exempted from national authorizations with respect to rules covered by the relevant 3CE framework. To the extent that such 3CE frameworks are capable of permitting market access, they avoid the need for third country firms to open a subsidiary in the EU.

Three general points should be made about the application of 3CE. First, it is not so much a general framework as a lattice of many specific regimes that operate together. Second, the scope of, goals for, and associated processes for making relevant determinations differ from regime to regime: the devil lies in the detail. The European Commission maintains a list of current 3CE determinations, which details 39 different equivalence regimes under 14

---

[14] Chris Brummer, *Soft Law and the Global Financial System: Rule Making in the 21st Century* (2nd edn, New York, CUP 2015).

[15] Armour et al (n6).

[16] See Sir Jon Cunliffe, 'Evidence on "Brexit and Financial Services"' to House of Lords Select Committee on the European Union Financial Affairs Sub-Committee (12 October 2016); Simon Gleeson, 'Evidence on "Brexit and Financial Services"' to House of Lords Select Committee on the European Union Financial Affairs Sub-Committee (14 September 2016).

[17] See Lucia Quaglia, 'The Politics of "Third Country Equivalence" in Post-crisis Financial Services Regulation in the European Union' (2015) 38 Western European Politics 167–184; Eilís Ferran, 'The UK as a Third Country Actor in EU Financial Services Regulation' (2017) 3 Journal of Financial Regulation 40–65; European Commission, 'EU Equivalence Decisions in Financial Services Policy: An Assessment' Commission Staff Working Document SWD (2017) 102 final.

different pieces of EU financial services legislation.[18] Third, 3CE is a moving target. New provisions are continually being added, and the way in which the 3CE processes are framed is also developing over time. In February 2017, the Commission announced a review of the way in which 3CE regimes operate. The associated Commission Staff Working Document studiously avoids mentioning Brexit, but, perhaps ominously for the UK, emphasises the importance of equivalence determinations as a means of ensuring financial stability and not simply open markets.[19] Together, these features make understanding the likely post-Brexit 3CE picture a complex and fast-changing endeavour. With these caveats in mind, it is worth making a few general observations about the likely operation of 3CE. We begin with the process of making a determination, and then turn to the scope of the relevant effects.

5. Determining equivalence: process

The key precondition to the application of a 3CE regime is that there must be an authoritative determination that the third country's regulatory regime is *equivalent* to the EU regime.[20] This is generally done by the Commission, increasingly following an assessment by the relevant European Supervisory Authority. The UK government has announced that it plans a wholesale enactment of all previously-binding EU law into domestic UK law. It follows that, at the point of exit, the UK will have in place a body of financial regulation that necessarily will be substantively equivalent to EU law.

There is a widely held fear that the process of determining equivalence may become politicized in the context of a messy Brexit negotiation. How politicization might creep in may be illustrated by imagining what would happen were the ECB to reinstate its 2011 policy of requiring euro-denominated transactions to be cleared within the Eurozone. As we have seen, once it is outside the EU, the UK would not be able to stop such a policy from being implemented. And yet, equally, it would have no binding obligation to comply with such a policy. Here is it is possible to see there might be pressure on the Commission to treat a failure by the UK to comply with such a policy as grounds for non-'equivalence'.

---

[18] European Commission, 'Equivalence Decisions Taken by the European Commission (as at 21/12/2016)' (2016) <https://ec.europa.eu/info/sites/info/files/file_import/equivalence-table_en.pdf> accessed 8 June 2017.

[19] European Commission (n17).

[20] Markets in Financial Instruments Regulation ('MiFIR'), Arts 46(2)(a).

Table 2: Third countries for which equivalence determinations
have been made

Sector	Measure	G20 countries	Financial centres/ other
Banking	CRD IV/ CRR	Australia, Brazil, Canada, China, India, Indonesia, Japan, South Korea, Mexico, Saudi Arabia, South Africa, USA	Hong Kong, Singapore and Switzerland
Insurance	Solvency II	Australia, Brazil, Canada, Japan, Mexico, USA	Bermuda, Switzerland
Prospectuses	PD	Turkey	Israel
Credit Ratings	CRA Regulation	Argentina, Australia, Brazil, Canada, Japan, Mexico, USA	Hong Kong, Singapore
Derivatives (CCPs)	EMIR	Australia, Brazil, Canada, India, Japan, South Korea, Mexico, South Africa and the USA	Dubai, Hong Kong, New Zealand, Singapore, Switzerland and the UAE

Notes: CRD IV/CRR is Capital Requirements Directive IV 2013/36/EU and Capital Requirements Regulation (EU) No 575/2031; PD is Prospectus Directive 2003/71/EC; CRA Regulation is Credit Rating Agencies Regulation (EC) No 1060/2009, as amended by Regulation (EU) No 462/2013; EMIR is European Market Infrastructure Regulation (EU) No 658/2012.

Ironically, this fear of politicization likely under-appreciates the merits of leaving decisions to technocrats, which is precisely what the democratically opaque structure of the Commission, and *a fortiori* the delegation of the initial assessment to the European Supervisory Authorities ('ESAs'), is intended to achieve.[21] Table 2 shows the third countries for which equivalence determinations have been made by the Commission as regards a range of existing 3CE regimes. As can be seen, the list consists largely of subsets of G20 countries and international financial centres. Each of these countries has a common interest with the EU in the relevant sectors. While bureaucrats at the Commission are unlikely to feel much sympathy towards the UK, it would surely be inconsistent with both the EU's interests and the vision of the EU project for them to treat the UK appreciably differently to this list of existing partners. This means that moves, for example, to repatriate euro

---

[21] Moloney (n8).

clearing could not credibly be directed only against the UK, but would need to be of general application. As euros are also cleared in the US and Asian jurisdictions, this would likely trigger a round of costly retaliation.

A more plausible concern is whether the Commission will have completed the necessary equivalence determinations by the time the UK's 2-year Article 50 period is completed. Neither a third country, nor its firms, have any right to compel the Commission to start the process of making an equivalence determination, even if the third country would manifestly meet the criteria. For example, the very earliest equivalence decisions under EMIR – Australia, Hong Kong, and Singapore – took 2 years from when the legislation came into force, and it took 4 years for the EU to accept the equivalence of the US regime on central counterparties for derivatives.

A third concern relates to the future beyond the short term. Equivalence must be reviewed periodically, and an initial decision in favour of the UK may be withdrawn by the Commission at will. While the regimes will be equivalent on exit, they may rapidly diverge. The EU has produced new legislation governing the financial sector at an astonishing rate since the financial crisis. On ceasing to be hardwired into the system, the UK will rapidly fall behind unless it adopts a mechanism for automatic implementation of new EU financial regulation initiatives into domestic law. However, the increasing growth in coordination of international standard-setting through the FSB means that if such activity continues, and the UK maintains strong links in that forum,[22] the UK may be able to continue to influence the regulatory agenda – no longer through the EU process directly, but at a level above the EU.

6. What benefits would equivalence confer?

If the process of third-country equivalence is workable, what would be the scope of its effect? As we shall see, there is alignment between the breadth of 3CE regimes and the areas in which the EU's financial sector currently labours under a comparative disadvantage. The 3CE regimes are most extensive for wholesale financial markets, and least extensive for retail markets and commercial banking, with insurance falling in between.[23]

a) Retail markets

Retail markets comprise those financial products and services that may legally be offered to retail investors or consumers. There is very little scope for 3CE in retail financial products: not for banking services, nor for investment funds or products, nor for investment advice, nor even brokerage

---

[22] Mark Carney, the Governor of the Bank of England, is currently also Chair of the FSB.

[23] See, generally, Freshfields Bruckhaus Deringer, 'The Legal Impact of Brexit on the UK-Based Financial Services Sector' (2017) Report commissioned by TheCityUK <https://www.thecityuk.com/research/the-legal-impact-of-brexit-on-the-uk-based-financial-services-sector/> accessed 8 June 2017.

services. This reflects in part the political sensitivity of access to EU retail investors, and in part the fact that there is, even within the EU, little in the way of cross-border retail financial service provision.

b) Commercial banking

EU legislation on banking regulation provides only very limited scope for 3CE, and does not provide for any direct access to the EU by third-country firms. There are 3CE provisions providing for coordination of supervision and for 'prudential equivalence'. However, none of these 3CE frameworks covers the provision of lending services by third-country banks within the EU. Nor do they cover the operation of payment systems, or the operation of bank resolution and insolvency.

As we saw, banking is currently responsible for over half of the UK's intra-EU exports of financial services. This would likely be substantially impaired by hard Brexit, absent a change in the 3CE regime. City practitioners quantify the at-risk revenues at £20 billion – that is, most of the intra-EU exports detailed in Table 1. However, a significant component of the activity listed in Table 1 as 'banking' – perhaps as much as a third – could be capable of falling within 3CE regimes for wholesale markets.[24] The big question going forward would be the extent to which the resources currently supporting intra-EU banking in the UK could be redeployed to other areas such as wholesale markets. Most obviously at risk would be the component of the UK banking sector made up of non-EU-headquartered banks that have established a UK subsidiary in order to benefit from the EU banking passport. These firms, which in 2015 had UK assets of £1.32 billion, or 14 per cent of the UK banking sector, would see their reason for being in the UK vanish.[25] Their parent companies would likely relocate these operations to other EU member states, such as Ireland or Luxembourg.

c) Insurance

EU insurance legislation contains an earlier and less elaborate 3CE framework than is featured in many subsequent legislative instruments. This reflects the fact that disagreements between the US and Europe over insurance regulation mean that there is not yet international consensus in the area,[26] so the drivers for change discussed above have had less effect.

---

[24] The Oliver Wyman data include within 'banking' subcomponents of 'investment banking' and 'sales and trading', accounting respectively for 10 per cent and 26 per cent of total banking revenues (see Oliver Wyman (n1) 4). Most of these activities could be conducted within the remit of the MiFID II 3CE, discussed below. Unfortunately, the intra-EU components of these activities are not reported.

[25] Non-EU firms make a particularly significant contribution to the conduct of wholesale banking activity in London—approximately half of such activity (André Sapir, Dirk Shoenmaker and Nicolas Véron, 'Making the Best of Brexit for the EU27 Financial System' (2017) 1 Bruegel Policy Brief Issue, 1–8). However, many of the wholesale banking activities, as explained in the text, may be able to benefit from 3CE (see also Freshfields Bruckhaus Deringer (n23)). Most at risk of repatriation are non-EU commercial banks.

[26] Huw Evans, 'Evidence on "Brexit and Financial Services"' to House of Lords Select Committee on the European Union Financial Affairs Sub-Committee (12 October 2016).

Like banking, the insurance 3CE provisions focus on supervisory coordination, especially the recognition of third-country group supervision arrangements. Analogously to banking, it does not provide a framework for the provision of insurance services by third-country firms into the EU. However, it does do so for reinsurance, through providing a 3CE mechanism for reinsurance supervision. Unlike banking, the insurance industry already largely operates through subsidiaries in other European jurisdictions.[27] This means that the sector would have less to lose from Brexit.

d) Wholesale financial markets

Most importantly, the MiFID II legislation coming into force at the beginning of 2018 (the Markets in Financial Instruments Directive II and associated Regulation) will introduce a so-called 'third-country passport'.[28] This will mean that eligible firms that register a branch in one EU member state will be able to provide investment services and activities to sophisticated clients throughout the EU without any need for further authorization.[29]

The third-country passport will only cover transactions with sophisticated clients.[30] For such persons, it will extend to all core investment banking activity, including brokerage, underwriting, mergers and acquisitions ('M&A') advisory work, market making, and proprietary trading.[31] It will not, however, cover regular commercial lending, except insofar as this constitutes an 'ancillary service' to investment services and activities of these sorts.[32] A potential drawback for firms using this regime is that they must offer clients the opportunity to have any legal disputes arising resolved in an EU member state.[33]

Alongside MiFID II, there is already in place a series of 3CE frameworks under regulations introduced to govern various aspects of 'market infrastructure', including derivatives trading (on-exchange) and clearing (for OTC derivatives), securities financing transaction trade repositories and reporting requirements, and central securities depositaries. There is also, in

---

[27] Vicenzo Scarpetta and Stephen Booth, 'How the UK's Financial Services Sector Can Continue Thriving After Brexit' Open Europe Report 10/2016 <http://2ihmoy1d3-v7630ar9h2rsglp.wpengine.netdna-cdn.com/wp-content/uploads/2016/10/0627_Digital_Pages-Open_Europe_Intel-Thriving_after_Brexit-V1.pdf?emailid=577bc2bcc0350c0300f8b09d&ft-camp=crm/email//nbe/Brexit/product> accessed 8 June 2017.

[28] Markets in Financial Instruments Directive II ('MiFID II') and Markets in Financial Instruments Regulation ('MiFIR').

[29] There will be registration requirements associated with establishing such a branch (MiFID II, Art 39), including minimum capital requirements and the need for a bilateral cooperation agreement between the third country and the EU 'home branch' NCA.

[30] MiFIR, Art 46(5).

[31] MiFID II Annex I, Section A. See also *ibid*, Section B.

[32] This means that while prime brokerage lending would be covered (as the loan is to a brokerage client to facilitate trading), the provision of loans to finance an M&A transaction would not be (whereas underwriting a junk bond issue to finance an M&A transaction would be covered).

[33] MiFIR, Art 46(6).

theory, a parallel 3CE regime for alternative investment fund managers (covering all non-retail investment funds), although it has not yet been implemented.

7. Conclusion

Given the parties' negotiating stances, Brexit will almost certainly spell the end of the EU passporting regime for UK-based financial services firms. The best outcome for the UK, absent breaking the deadlock on free movement, would be for a negotiated agreement on financial services that offers something more than the patchwork of 3CE provisions discussed above. The UK would want such an agreement to (i) provide a more enduring foundation for access by its firms than a unilateral equivalence determination by the Commission; (ii) to cover, in addition to wholesale markets, in order of priority, payment services, banking activity, and wholesale insurance. How far the UK gets towards this goal in the negotiations will likely depend at least in part on its outside option – reliance on 3CE.

The breadth of the 3CE regimes in wholesale markets matches the UK's comparative advantage, and the comparative disadvantage of the EU, as respects financial services. There is consequently a clear mutual interest for both the EU and the UK in continued connectivity using this framework. There are, however, real risks. The most immediate relate to the process of determining equivalence. The logistics are such that the necessary assessments by the Commission are unlikely to be completed by March 2019. Moreover, despite its technocratic composition, the Commission may to some degree be influenced in its conduct of these assessments by other factors in the Brexit negotiations.

Even assuming 3CE determinations are achieved, there are further risks going forwards. First, the 3CE regime for wholesale markets could serve to open the UK up to competition from other third countries. If the 3CE regime permits US – and perhaps Asian-based – firms to provide such services into the EU, then the EU's need for UK wholesale services would be significantly weakened. The UK has breathing space here, at least as regards the US, because of the requirement for reciprocity of treatment that is included in recent 3CE regimes, including the very important MiFID II third-country passport. At present, there is no comparable mechanism by which EU firms offering investment services can obtain exemption from compliance with US regulation on the basis that the EU rules are equivalent.[34]

---

[34] Such 'substitute compliance' frameworks, as they are known in the US, currently only operate to a very limited extent in relation to derivatives and not at all for investment services 'inbound' to the US (see John C Coffee, Jr, 'Extraterritorial Financial Regulation: Why ET Can't Come Home' (2014) 99 Cornell L Rev 1259–1302; Alexey Artamonov, 'Cross-border Application of OTC Derivatives Rules: Revisiting the Substituted Compliance Approach' (2015) 1 (2) J Financ Regul 206–225; John Armour, Martin Bengtzen and Luca Enriques, 'Investor Choice in Global Securities Markets' in Merritt B Fox and Lawrence R Glosten (eds) *The New Special Study of the Securities Markets* (forthcoming)).

Second, the recent nationalistic turn in US politics bodes ill for the continued significance of the FSB and, with it, the UK's chances of influencing the EU from 'above'. The US has been an important player in ensuring the success of the FSB. Should the US, as seems likely, move from a role akin to global policeman for the FSB's standards – implicitly threatening non-compliant states – to one of open recalcitrance, then the FSB's credibility will be greatly undermined. A weakened FSB would reduce the UK's ability to influence EU regulation through this channel.

As a result, the worst-case outcomes might be very bad indeed, especially for the UK. It seems highly desirable that the parties agree a transition period pending at the very least completion of equivalence determinations and more usefully, the conclusion of a suitable bilateral agreement.

John Armour is the Hogan Lovells Professor of Law
and Finance at the University of Oxford.

Negotiating a Financial Services Deal: Politics, Preferences, and Predictions

Niamh Moloney

After months of discussion on potential European Union ('EU')/United Kingdom ('UK') access models for financial services,[1] the launch of the Article 50 exit process on 29 March 2017 with Prime Minister May's 'Article 50 letter' cleared the way for the negotiations.[2] Financial services are clearly a UK priority. The Article 50 letter specifically notes the need to cover financial services in a 'bold and ambitious' Free Trade Agreement. It also identifies the two issues which have dominated the financial services debate since the referendum: the need for the proposed new access arrangement to address EU/UK regulatory divergence (the letter refers to the 'evolution' of regulatory frameworks); and the need for related dispute resolution mechanisms (a reference to the difficulties posed by the jurisdiction of the Court of Justice over access arrangements, the removal of which is a 'redline' for Prime Minister May).

Whether or not the negotiations will lead to a Free Trade Agreement which meets the UK's market access objectives will be shaped by multiple and dynamic interests and preferences, and is impossible to predict at the time of writing. It is, however, clear, that EU political preferences, at European Council and Member State level, will be key and also that the preferences of the major EU institutions engaged should not be overlooked. This short outline note briefly comments on the EU institutional preferences and incentives which may shape the negotiations.

1. Protecting 'Single Market Technology'

Current EU indications suggest a strong commitment to the single market in financial services, to the single rulebook, and to the institutional governance arrangements of the European System of Financial Supervision, which sup-

---

[1] The comments presented in this short note are examined in detail in Kern Alexander, Catherine Barnard, Ellis Ferran, Andrew Lang, and Niamh Moloney, *Brexit and Financial Services: Law and Policy* (forthcoming, Hart Publishing 2018). The note is based on a short blog prepared by the author for March 2017 and is only very lightly updated to end May 2017 (see Niamh Moloney, 'Brexit Negotiations Series: "Negotiating a Financial Services Deal: Politics and Preferences" (*Oxford Business Law Blog*, 6 April 2017) <https://www.law.ox.ac.uk/business-law-blog/blog/2017/04/brexit-negotiations-series-'negotiating-financial-services-deal> accessed 31 May 2017).

[2] Letter from Theresa May to Donald Tusk (29 March 2017) <https://www.gov.uk/government/publications/prime-ministers-letter-to-donald-tusk-triggering-article-50> accessed 31 May 2017.

ports the single market in financial services. Even allowing for the change in political dynamics, which the election of President Macron in France may herald, there is little evidence of an entrepreneurial push for deeper euro area financial governance following the departure of the UK, which has been the strongest advocate for multi-currency financial governance.[3] Any such euro-area move could have generated political and institutional tensions and led to a cleavage between EU Member States and institutions to the UK's advantage. There is instead every indication of an EU concern to protect the governance technology which supports the single market in financial services and to make a clear distinction, accordingly, between single market 'membership' and 'access'.

For example, and from an institutional perspective, prior to the Brexit referendum the institutional tea-leaves could have been read as supporting the continued intensification and expansion of euro area financial governance beyond banking, particularly as the Single Supervisory Mechanism ('SSM') was becoming increasingly normalized. The centralization of euro area markets governance, for example, had been mooted, including by the 2015 Five Presidents' Report on Completing Economic and Monetary Union.[4] But any enthusiasm for new 'grand designs' in risk-sharing and in related institutional construction seems to be waning, at least for the short to medium term; progress on Banking Union's European Deposit Insurance Scheme and on its fiscal back-stop is slow. Risk reduction, not risk sharing, is the current focus of institutional attention, with the single market's single rulebook seen as the main vehicle for risk reduction. At the same time, there is some evidence of a concern, particularly in the European Parliament, to prevent the SSM from encroaching into single market governance.

Similarly, and from a regulatory governance perspective, the major package of bank regulation reforms proposed by the European Commission (the 'Commission') in November 2016[5] and the Commission's related November 2016 future reform agenda for financial regulation (which followed the 2015–2016 'stock take' of EU financial regulation)[6] both suggest a strong commitment to the EU's single rulebook governing the single market; paraphrasing Prime Minister May's 17 January 2017 'Lancaster House' speech on the UK's

---

[3] The protection of single market governance arrangements from euro area caucusing and preferences was a major theme of the 'New Settlement' which David Cameron agreed with the European Council prior to the referendum: Decision of the Heads of State or Government Meeting Within the European Council, Concerning a New Settlement for the United Kingdom with the European Union, European Council Meeting [2016] OJ CI 69/1.

[4] Jean-Claude Juncker, 'Completing Europe's Economic and Monetary Union – Report by Jean-Claude Juncker, in close cooperation with Donald Tusk, Jeroen Dijsselbloem, Mario Draghi and Martin Schulz' (*European Commission*, June 2015) <http://www.consilium.europa.eu/en/european-council/.../pdf/5-presidents-report-en_pdf/> accessed 31 May 2017.

[5] Which include proposals for reforms to the 2013 Capital Requirements Directive IV/ Capital Requirements Regulation.

[6] European Commission, 'Communication on Call for Evidence – EU Regulatory Framework for Financial Services' COM (2016) 855 final.

negotiating objectives,[7] the EU will likely 'bend more sharply to uniformity' in relation to regulatory governance. The need for regulatory flexibility and calibration within the single rulebook is increasingly being acknowledged, but EU-level proportionality mechanisms, directed to the specificities of different firms and market segments, and not to national options and derogations, appear to be the adjustment mechanism of choice.

In parallel, there appears to be new appetite for strengthening the single market's European Supervisory Authorities ('ESAs') which perform an array of quasi-regulatory and supervisory/coordination activities within the European System of Financial Supervision. The Commission's 21 March 2017 consultation on the future of the ESAs is noticeably more sympathetic to the possibility of additional supervisory powers being conferred on the ESAs than the Commission has been in the past; its referencing of the potential need for supervisory changes following the UK withdrawal may be a straw in the wind indicating stronger single market institutional governance.[8] In particular, while, at the time of this note, the future location of the supervision of central clearing counterparties ('CCPs') is uncertain, the need to address the governance risks posed by the off-shore location in the UK of, in some clearing segments, over 70 % of euro-denominated clearing following the UK withdrawal looks set to lead to some form of re-ordering of EU-level supervision and, possibly, to a related empowerment of the European Securities and Markets Authority ('ESMA'), based on the Commission's 4 May 2017 note.[9]

These recent indications all suggest a commitment to reinforcing and enhancing the technology of single market financial governance, on which the EU has expended considerable political and institutional capital since the financial crisis, which is now beginning to mature and stabilize, and which the EU can be expected to protect. Any bespoke equivalence/market access arrangements to be contained in an EU/UK Free Trade Agreement, as signalled in the UK's Article 50 letter, would, however, operate outside this hard-fought single market technology: the current third country/equivalence/access arrangements for financial services are based on single market law and governance, including Court of Justice oversight and advisory/supervisory engagement by ESMA. The UK's aspirations could accordingly struggle to be realized – although there may be some wiggle room, from the UK side, in the Article 50 letter's acknowledgement of the need to address dispute resolution and to manage regulatory evolution (which may be a nod towards some form of *de facto* shadowing in the UK of the single rulebook). The

---

[7] Theresa May, 'Speech' (Lancaster House, 17 January 2017) <https://www.gov.uk/government/speeches/the-governments-negotiating-objectives-for-exiting-the-eu-pm-speech> accessed 31 May 2017.

[8] European Commission, 'Public Consultation on the Operations of the European Supervisory Authorities' (*European Commission*, 21 March 2017) <https://ec.europa.eu/info/consultations/public-consultation-operations-european-supervisory-authorities_en> accessed 31 May 2017.

[9] European Commission, 'Responding to Challenges for Critical Market Infrastructure and Further Developing the Capital Markets Union' COM(2017) 225 final.

Negotiation Guidelines issued by the European Council on 29 April 2017, however, do not suggest the EU will give way on Court of Justice oversight. The Guidelines also indicate that the EU will seek to protect its financial governance arrangements. The Guidelines note, for example, that 'the Union will preserve its autonomy as regards its decision-making as well as the role of the Court of Justice of the European Union.'[10] Similarly, there have been signals from the European Parliament that it would oppose any future EU/ UK agreement which contained piecemeal or sectoral provisions, including with respect to financial services, and that it sees the UK as falling under the third country regime provided for in EU legislation on withdrawal.[11] The difficult negotiations on the Single Resolution Mechanism provide an earlier and cautionary tale: the European Parliament was fiercely opposed to the Intergovernmental Agreement which operates outside single market governance being used to govern the Mechanism's funding.

2. Institutional Preferences

The European Parliament will be a key player in the negotiations and, since the financial crisis era, it has developed strong preferences and technical capacity on financial market governance. Prior to the Brexit referendum, it was becoming increasingly interested in the EU's engagement with global financial governance, calling for greater oversight of how this was carried out, particularly of the Commission, which traditionally represents the EU in international governance settings.[12] The Parliament's opposition to any disruption to single market arrangements is already clear from its April 2017 Resolution on the negotiations. Further, and from an institutional balance perspective, it may not support bespoke EU/UK arrangements which lead to a significant empowerment of the Commission. The Parliament is also likely to have distinct views on the design of any new supervisory arrangements. One of the more intractable elements of any bespoke EU/UK deal on financial services and of the access debate, generally, is likely to be the organization of EU supervision of any UK-located services provided into the

---

[10] European Council, 'Article 50 Guidelines Following the UK's Notification under Article 50 TFEU' (*Press Release 220/17*, 29 April 2017) <http://www.consilium.europa.eu/en/press/press-releases/2017/04/29-euco-brexit-guidelines/> accessed 31 May 2017.

[11] European Parliament, 'Resolution on Negotiations with the UK following its Notification that it intends to Withdraw from the EU' 2017/2593(RSP). The Resolution warns, for example, that any bilateral UK/Member State agreement involving 'any privileged access to the internal market for United Kingdom-based financial institutions at the expense of the Union's regulatory framework or to the status of EU 27 citizens in the United Kingdom or vice versa' would breach the Treaties. It also 'opposes any future agreement between the European Union and the United Kingdom that would contain piecemeal or sectorial provisions, including with respect to financial services, providing United Kingdom-based undertakings with preferential access to the internal market and/or the customs union' and 'underlines that after its withdrawal the United Kingdom will fall under the third-country regime provided for in Union legislation.'

[12] European Parliament, 'Resolution of 12 April 2016 on the EU Role in the Framework of International, Financial, Monetary and Regulatory Institutions and Bodies' 2015/2060(INI).

EU 27 market – in particular the capital market services in which the UK dominates. The EU will be concerned to ensure its interests (whether competitive, financial-stability-oriented, or otherwise) are protected in relation to the supervision of UK actors in the EU market. There is a spectrum of potential design options, from full-scale repatriation of activities to the EU (typically associated with euro-denominated clearing and CCPs) to reliance on UK supervision. The Parliament has traditionally been a supporter of EU-level supervision through the ESAs and may require some form of EU-led supervision of UK firm activities in the EU.

The Commission can also be expected to protect single market governance arrangements, notably the equivalence regime which governs aspects of third country access to the EU financial market. Its delicately-timed 27 February 2017 report on equivalence has a chilly tone, noting that equivalence arrangements are not a tool for trade liberalization, but for protecting the stability of the EU market.[13] The report does not suggest an appetite for major change to the current equivalence regime and contains two important signals which caution against predictions of new, liberal approaches to access, whether in an EU/UK Free Trade Agreement, or otherwise: the Commission seeks a more finely-tuned, proportionate, risk-based approach to equivalence, under which markets of more systemic relevance to the EU would receive more attention; and plans to engage in more monitoring of third country supervision.

Finally, the role of the ESAs should not be overlooked, given their technocratic capacity and growing influence on EU financial governance; in particular, ESMA can be identified as an important institutional actor in relation to the Brexit negotiations, not least given its potential as a location for EU-level supervision and/or coordination relating to UK-located capital market business and its experience with equivalence-related decision-making and supervisory coordination. ESMA Chair Maijoor has warned of the potential risks to the EU from reliance on third country supervision and suggested (in the context of third country CCP access to the EU – which is managed in the main through ESMA which registers third country CCPs) that the EU 'is an island of third country reliance,' relying on third country (home) supervision in a world in which cross-border access usually means that supervision in the relevant host market (here the EU) follows.[14] ESMA is, by now, an experienced supervisor in certain capital market segments (credit rating agencies and trade repositories) and may emerge from the Brexit negotiation period with enhanced powers, whether in relation to the supervision of third country actors, equivalence determinations, or coordination with the global market, including the UK, more generally.

---

[13] European Commission, 'EU Equivalence Decisions in Financial Service Policy: an assessment' SWD(2017) 102 final.

[14] Steven Maijoor, 'Speech' (ALDE Party Seminar on the Review of the ESAs, European Parliament, 8 February 2017) <https://www.esma.europa.eu/press-news/esma-news/steven-maijoors-address-alde-seminar-review-european-supervisory-authorities> accessed 31 May 2017.

Prediction of how the Brexit negotiations will proceed is a fraught business. But overall, this short note suggests that the attachment of the EU to the current single market governance arrangements can be expected to shape its approach to the negotiations. This attachment cautions against predictions of radically different arrangements for UK access to the current single-market-oriented, equivalence-based system, whether in a Free Trade Agreement or otherwise.

Niamh Moloney is Professor at the Law Department of the London School of Economics and Political Science.

Implications of Brexit For Private Equity and Private Equity-Backed Firms[1]

Mark Soundy

I am probably going to be the least interesting panelist in any of today's sessions because, in the longer term, it seems very unlikely that Brexit (or, for that matter, Nexit or Frexit, or Quitaly) will have any significantly adverse impact on Private Equity. Plus ça change, frankly.

I am a Private Equity lawyer at Goodwin, one of the world's leading Private Equity law firms. I have been doing Private Equity for 30 years – pretty much right from the start of it in the United Kingdom ('UK') – and, in the context of this particular talk, there are three things I would note about the evolution of Private Equity during that time:

First, Private Equity folks are remarkably creative and inventive. They love a challenge: in fact, the best of them make the most money in those circumstances. They see Brexit as a moneymaking opportunity, just like the Black Monday Crash of 1987, the Dotcom Bubble Burst of 2000, the Global Financial Crisis of 2007-8, the election of Donald Trump, etc.

Second, Private Equity is a truly international business. Yes, there are some Private Equity investors who are very UK-centric and who focus on investing principally in UK businesses, but very few UK businesses today operate solely in the UK. Most are European, or even more international in their reach. Take our client Bridgepoint, a leading mid-market European Private Equity house: they operate in over 80 different jurisdictions, as a result of their investments. What is happening as a result of Brexit in the UK, even in Europe, is only one (ever decreasing) aspect of their business.

Third, a number of Private Equity houses have diversified into alternative asset managers. Not only do they invest in Private Equity, they also invest in Real Estate, in Infrastructure, in Debt, etc. Indeed, the fundamentals of what follows apply more widely than to just the Private Equity asset class, and that softens the impact of Brexit.

In my contribution, I will examine two aspects of Private Equity – (i) Private Equity fund-raising; and (ii) Private Equity investing – but, first, let me start by laying down a few interesting and pertinent facts about the Private Equity industry in the UK and in the rest of the European Union ('rEU'), based on statistics published by the UK's voice of Private Equity: the British Venture Capital Association (the 'BVCA'). Over the last 5 years, those Private Equity

---

[1] This article is based on the author's contribution at the 'Negotiating Brexit' conference that took place in Oxford on 17 March 2017.

41

funds who are members of the BVCA have invested more than £27bn in around 4,000 UK-based businesses. Currently, UK-based Private Equity funds back some 3,000 businesses employing over 900,000 people (on a full-time basis) around the world, of which 40 % are in the UK and 30 % are in the rEU.

Looking at the two distinct aspects of Private Equity, over the last 3 years, it should be noted that, with regard to fund-raising, 18 % of funds raised by UK-based funds were from rEU countries, and, with regard to investing, 40 % of UK-based fund investment activity was in companies based in the rEU. It seems, by any measure, that Private Equity is important to the UK and to the rEU; and that the rEU is important to UK-based Private Equity.

So, what are the implications of Brexit for Private Equity fund-raising? Most of the chatter in this area has been around (i) regulatory changes effectively preventing UK-based funds from attracting investors from the rEU (the source of 18 % of their funds over the last 3 years); and (ii) tax changes, especially withholding tax preventing or restricting the up-streaming of dividends and interest within portfolio company groups. The fact that investors suffer more (indirect) tax on these investments will ultimately impact investor returns.

If regulatory, tax, or any other changes make UK-based Private Equity significantly less attractive, guess what: those UK-based Private Equity funds will simply de-camp and move their operations elsewhere. These funds are not like big investment banks and retail banks: they employ relatively few back-office staff and their investment professionals are usually multi-cultural, multi-lingual people from far and wide who enjoy living in London. But it's the shops, restaurants, culture, and schools that attract them to London, far more than the smooth and efficient workings of the current UK/rEU regulatory regime. If they have to, they will simply go and live in Geneva, or Frankfurt, or Dublin – indeed, many London-based Private Equity funds already have offices and established operations elsewhere in Europe. Our Private Equity fund clients are already contingency planning for this. They tell us that, based on the current Brexit timetable, they need to decide what to do in around six months' time so that, if necessary, they can transition away from the UK with minimal disruption to their businesses. If the post-Brexit landscape for Private Equity is not clear by then, surely the business imperative will be to seek greater certainty by leaving the UK (and its bickering politicians) behind.

And what are the implications of Brexit for Private Equity investing? In the longer-term, it looks as if Brexit will have very little effect (although businesses in certain geographies or sectors may become more, or less attractive). Today, the uncertainties of Brexit are making it harder to do deals, and, particularly, to conduct due diligence and to value potential investments. But a typical Private Equity fund is structured with a 10-year lifespan comprising an initial period of 5 years to invest the fund and then a subsequent 5 years to realise those investments. So, Private Equity funds cannot afford to sit on their hands for too long: they have to put their money to work. And, today, with more 'dry powder' (ie, more money committed to Private Equity funds and waiting to be invested) across the globe than ever before, there is huge pressure to invest and Private Equity simply cannot ignore the UK or the rEU, despite Brexit uncertainty.

That is the reason why, even in the teeth of Brexit, we were still doing deals for our Private Equity clients. Very shortly after the Brexit referendum, for example, we advised a Private Equity fund on its investment in an online food delivery company (Deliveroo). This target is a very British business, although it is growing very rapidly across Europe and even more internationally. It was an unusual investment for our client (particularly because they were only taking a minority stake), and I was sure, that immediately post-Brexit, they would call the whole thing off. But they didn't: they merely adjusted their pricing (by a very unscientific 3 %) and closed the deal. We also advised another Private Equity fund on the realization of its investment in a business manufacturing crisps (Tyrrells). This was another very British target business, although, again, one that is growing internationally. Again, I was sure that Brexit would immediately scotch the deal. But no: the business was sold, for a mouth-watering price, to a United States ('US') strategic buyer who, because of Brexit, was able to get more bang for its buck and who, in any event, was more interested in leveraging the brand State-side than in Europe.

Private Equity, at least in the mid-market and upwards, needs 'leverage' (ie, money borrowed by the businesses that Private Equity funds buy) in order to enhance the returns on their investments. So, is Private Equity deal-doing likely to be adversely affected by the Brexit uncertainties surrounding, for example, the European banking industry? No, I do not think so. Many of the European banks have still not fully recovered from the Global Financial Crisis of 2007–2008. As a result, for quite some time now, Private Equity has looked elsewhere for its life-giving leverage: and abundant debt has been found in the US markets (what is known as the rise of Term Loan B), in the High Yield debt capital markets, and coming from specialist Alternative Debt Providers.

One last thought: one of the things that distinguishes a Private Equity deal from a traditional mergers and acquisitions ('M&A') deal is that a Private Equity fund (in contrast to a corporate buyer) will typically be looking to realise (or 'exit') its investment within 3–5 years. So, at the time when such funds make their Private Equity investments, they are already looking ahead to what that target business might look like, and where the markets might be, around that time horizon. As they crystal ball gaze, we hear increasing concerns about another looming economic downturn, which could hit in the next two years. Given the Brexit timings and uncertainties we have been hearing about, it could be that a perfect storm is brewing.

Mark Soundy is a partner
in Goodwin's Private Equity Group.

A Brexit Deal for Financial Services

Wolf-Georg Ringe

Among participants in the global financial market, Brexit is commonly painted as an almost Apocalypse-like scenario. The threat of a British exit from the European Union ('EU') arguably involves a significant disruption to financial integration in Europe, will threaten the pre-eminence of London as a global financial centre, and will impose significant costs on all market participants.

This short contribution takes a different position on the significance of Brexit for the European financial market.[1] I argue that, different from the public perception, the impact of Brexit for financial services will be minimal, if not irrelevant.[2] This view is grounded on the economic stakes for both sides, the United Kingdom ('UK') and the EU27, in retaining the benefits of access to the European Single Market for financial services. Given a combination of joint economic interests and political forces, a likely outcome of the Brexit negotiations will be a solution that formally satisfies the 2016 referendum result, but in substance keeps Britain closely involved in the EU financial market.

This hypothesis gains further support from historical examples in EU financial market integration that saw ingenious creativity at work in facilitating a desired outcome within the existing convoluted legal framework. These past experiences lead us to predict a similar approach being used for accommodating Brexit. In other words, whilst Brexit will be delivered *in form*, a separate agreement may replace the economic benefits of market access *in substance*.

This chapter contributes to the debate of 'Negotiating Brexit' by discussing several alternatives of *how* such a deal could look like. In declining order of preference, three scenarios are discussed: continued market access, third-country equivalence, and private ordering.

1. Continued Single Market access

Following the logic of the introduction, a tailor-made agreement between the UK and the EU27 guaranteeing continued Single Market access for financial services is the most likely scenario going forward. This would ensure that, on

---

[1] For an extended version of this chapter, see Wolf-Georg Ringe, 'The Irrelevance of Brexit for the European Financial Market', Oxford Legal Studies Research Paper No 10/2017 <http://ssrn.com/abstract=2902715> accessed 13 June 2017.

[2] ibid.

the one hand, the UK is formally leaving the bloc and thereby honouring the outcome of the referendum, and, on the other hand, still retains access to the Single Market in substance.

As a *quid pro quo*, it appears likely that the UK government will have to give ground on its position towards limiting immigration.[3] It is to be assumed that such a concession will officially be made with reluctance – but, in secret, the government is aware of the fact that such immigration is of actual benefit to the UK economy. The supply of workers and students from the EU has helped the UK grow faster than any other Member State in the past. To avoid suffocating the domestic industry, UK officials have already indicated that they may let in financial-services employees.[4] For example, Philip Hammond, the UK Chancellor of the Exchequer, openly discussed the possibility of granting special work permit exemptions to EU citizens working in financial services.[5] In terms of legal design, different variations are possible, depending on the bargaining power and negotiation outcome. Either the UK opts out from free movement, but allows a number of back-exceptions, or the UK remains subject to free movement but is allowed to deviate in a number of pre-defined areas. In substance, both approaches would probably yield very similar outcomes.

The result would be a bespoke agreement between the UK and the EU, not entirely dissimilar from the relationship between Switzerland and the EU. A far-reaching Single Market access for the UK appears to be the optimal solution. Political forces and populist influence on both sides of the Channel may, however, jeopardise this outcome.

A specific concept along these lines is a so-called 'Continental Partnership', proposed in a recent Bruegel policy paper. This is the idea of an idiosyncratic and innovative relationship between the UK and the EU resting on the UK's participation in a series of selected common policies consistent with access to the Single Market.[6] Although the details obviously need to be worked out, this idea may helpfully inform the debate and serve as a focal point and role model for future collaboration.

2. Equivalence and third-country passport

If full market membership for the financial industry cannot be successfully negotiated, a second best scenario is conceivable. Such a Plan B would assume that the UK counts as a 'third country' for EU financial regulation;

---

[3] Editors, 'The Road to Brexit' *The Economist* (8 October 2016) <http://www.economist.com/news/leaders/21708257-britains-prime-minister-must-resist-her-partys-dangerous-instincts-road-brexit> accessed 13 June 2017.

[4] ibid.

[5] George Parker and James Blitz, 'Hammond draws fire for Brexit caution' *Financial Times* (18 October 2016) 3.

[6] Jean Pisani-Ferry et al, 'Europe after Brexit: A proposal for a continental partnership' (25 August 2016) <http://bruegel.org/2016/08/europe-after-brexit-a-proposal-for-a-continental-partnership/> accessed 13 June 2017.

as such, the UK could still rely on being classified as an 'equivalent' legal system and thereby profit from a third country passport under relevant EU legislation.[7]

The EU utilises an equivalence test in many areas to reduce overlaps and capital costs for EU institutions that comply with rules in other countries,[8] and the UK places high hopes on this system as a fall-back position, or 'safety net'. There are a number of problems attached to using a third-country status for the Single Market, however.

The first issue is that third-country passporting rights tend to be restricted to wholesale financial services, whereas marketing of services to retail customers is typically not allowed. Thus, equivalence does not cover some core banking activities such as deposit taking and cross-border lending. This might not be a serious obstacle in practice, as the UK financial industry is arguably mostly focused on wholesale markets anyhow, and wholesale markets are the more lucrative part of the market overall.[9]

But two other considerations may make third-country access less palatable. First, the availability of third-country access is rather patchy. A number of pieces of EU legislation do include the principle, but others do not. For example, the legal framework for Undertakings for the Collective Investment of Transferable Securities ('UCITS') (mutual funds) in the EU does not allow third country passporting at all.[10] Even where it exists, the requirements and thresholds vary. This may jeopardise the possibility of a holistic Single Market access for the entirety of the UK financial sector. For example, in the field of hedge funds' access to the European market, whilst the relevant piece of EU legislation (the Alternative Investment Fund Managers Directive or 'AIFMD')[11] in theory provides for an equivalence rule, the Commission has never used it to date – and it does not seem inclined to do so.[12]

Even more serious is the risk of *political* exploitation attached to the vetting process steered by the European Commission (the 'Commission'). The

---

[7] See European Parliament, Directorate-General for Internal Policies/Economic Governance Support Unit, *Briefing: Third-country equivalence in EU banking legislation* (7 November 2016) <http://www.europarl.europa.eu/RegData/etudes/BRIE/2016/587369/IPOL_-BRI(2016)587369_EN.pdf> accessed 13 June 2017.

[8] Eilis Ferran, 'The UK as a Third Country Actor in EU Financial Services Regulation' (2017) 3 Journal of Financial Regulation 40.

[9] European Parliament Economic Governance Support Unit, *Briefing – Brexit: the United-Kingdom and EU financial services* (9 December 2016) 3–4 <http://www.europarl.europa.eu/RegData/etudes/BRIE/2016/587384/IPOL_BRI(2016)587384_EN.pdf> accessed 13 June 2017.

[10] Other examples of legal acts that do not provide for a passport are Capital Requirements Directive IV (comprising Capital Requirements Directive (Directive 2013/36/EU) and Capital Requirements Regulation (Regulation (EU) No 575/2013) and (in parts) Solvency II (Directive 2009/138/EC).

[11] European Parliament and Council, Directive 2011/61/EU of 8 June 2011 on Alternative Investment Fund Managers (2011) OJEU L174/1.

[12] Sean Tuffy, 'Hedge funds in the UK need a hard-Brexit contingency plan' Financial Times (5 December 2016) FTfm9.

Commission is *de facto* the sole body responsible for assessing whether a third country system really is 'equivalent' to EU standards. Given that the UK has long been an EU member and has faithfully implemented all of EU financial legislation over past decades, one would assume that the UK must be the paradigm example of an 'equivalent' jurisdiction. However, the risk remains that the equivalence decision is hijacked for political motives, unrelated to substantial reasons. Unlikely genuine Single Market access, equivalence is not an entitlement, but a privilege, which can be unilaterally withdrawn by the European Commission at short notice.[13]

We already see signs of political tactics over equivalence emerging right now, before the UK has even left: the EU recently initiated a process to review the equivalence regime overall, with a view of streamlining the process and toughening the approval criteria, in particular for systemically important financial institutions.[14] In its recent reflection document on the equivalence process, the European Commission uses remarkable strong rhetoric to under-line the fact that equivalence is primarily an instrument in the interest of the EU, and may only indirectly benefit the third country too.[15] Further, the Commission insists that '[e]quivalence is not a vehicle for liberalising inter-national trade' and '[t]he [equivalence] decision is a unilateral and discre-tionary act of the EU, both for its adoption and any possible amendment or repeal'.[16] This suggests that equivalence may be a rather unreliable last resort indeed. Reportedly, EU officials are already wary of setting precedents for Brexit when deciding about the equivalence with third countries today.[17]

Add to this the general thrust of Brexit: the perceived goal is to be precisely freed from EU legislation, and to reverse EU rules where possible. This could mean that every step of the UK legal order away from the EU acquis could be interpreted – or serve as a pretext – that the UK regulatory and supervisory standards are *not* equivalent (any more) to the EU legal order. Moreover, if the EU financial laws change over time, the UK would have to constantly adapt its own legislation to maintain continued market access for its financial services sector. This would be a politically very daunting exercise.

The only relief could come from a legally binding agreement between the third country and the EU that the former's rules are deemed equivalent.[18]

---

[13] Jonathan Ford, 'Brexit equivalence deal could spare City pain of Morton's fork' *Financial Times* (12 December 2016) 20.

[14] Alex Barker and Jim Brunsden, 'EU review casts doubt on City's hopes for "equiva-lence" as Brexit last resort' *Financial Times* (7 November 2016) 1.

[15] European Commission, Commission Staff Working Document – EU equivalence decisions in financial services policy: an assessment (27 February 2017) SWD (2017) 102 final.

[16] ibid.

[17] Barker and Brunsden (n14) 3.

[18] John Armour, 'Brexit and Financial Services', (2017) 33 Oxford Review of Economic Policy S54. See, for example, the 'expanded equivalence' proposal made by Barnabas Reynolds, *A Blueprint for Brexit: The Future of Global Financial Services and Markets in the UK* (Politeia Report 2016).

However, it is uncertain whether such an agreement is acceptable to the EU.[19] In any case, it would take a long time to negotiate, and firms may have to endure significant uncertainty during this long period. For example, it took the EU four years to negotiate a recent agreement with the United States Commodity Futures Trading Commission ('CFTC') on the equivalence of central counterparty clearing.[20] Therefore, an interim deal or transition agreement could at least ensure 'equivalence' for UK financial services standards so that the City firms could make use of the third country passport until the question is settled.

3. Private solutions

Were the UK and the EU to fail reaching an agreement, and the UK ceases to be a Member State by way of a 'hard' Brexit, private solutions by market participants are to be expected. Financial services providers would almost certainly pursue some strategy to mitigate the loss of passporting rights in the absence of a political deal.

An open question is whether individual firms could gain market access by volunteering to be subject to EU rules. The regulatory concept of 'voluntarism' may grant individual third-country firms access to local markets where these firms voluntarily commit to comply with local rules.[21] The 'beauty' of such an approach would be that it could be achieved in the absence of any political deal.

Importantly, however, such regimes currently only exist in some singular parts of the financial regulation framework, and only on the national level – not for the EU as a whole.[22] That is to say that, at best, UK firms may privately gain access to one particular area, in one particular jurisdiction, by striking an individual deal directly with another EU country. Further, EU law sometimes imposes limits on such national deals: for example, Article 54 of MIFIR permits such national regimes only for three years after an equivalence assessment. It does not appear, therefore, that such agreements would offer a stable perspective of market access for City firms. They would probably be rather piecemeal, complex and costly, and very much dependent on the goodwill of individual countries.

In reality, instead, UK financial firms may only truly secure Single Market access by way of setting up a subsidiary in one of the EU27 Member States

---

[19] For a critical comment, see Martin Wolf, 'A post-Brexit transition must be the priority' *Financial Times* (30 November 2016) 13.

[20] See Silla Brush and Benjamin Bain, 'EU Banks Closer to $5 Billion Respite With SEC Clearing Rule' *Bloomberg* (28 September 2016) <https://www.bloomberg.com/news/articles/2016-09-28/eu-banks-eye-5-billion-capital-reprieve-as-sec-votes-on-rules> accessed 13 June 2017.

[21] Jonathan Ford, 'City probes ways to access EU market after Brexit', *Financial Times* (London, 11 April 2017) 3.

[22] One example is the UK concept of 'overseas persons exclusion' under Financial Services and Markets Act 2000 (Regulated Activities) Order 2001 Article 72.

which could provide financial services as a separately regulated and capitalised legal entity.

However, such a move would not be a cost-free exercise. The EU financial legal framework has specific provisions to ensure that a subsidiary does not become a letterbox entity, where the company exists on paper and the work is done elsewhere.[23] In the case of banking, the subsidiary would require separate capitalisation, separate staff, and supervision by the host Member State.

Chances are that some large banking groups already have an EU subsidiary in place. For example, Credit Suisse CEO Tidjane Thiam explained that (despite substantial costs) the Swiss bank is in a 'reasonable position' to deal with any Brexit outcome thanks to its existing subsidiaries in Dublin and Luxembourg.[24] Likewise, Standard Chartered has announced plans to establish a new EU subsidiary in Frankfurt, citing the pre-existence of an office and staff there.[25]

These two statements reveal an important point of information: size matters. Whereas large financial services groups are likely to already have an EU27-based subsidiary in place, or to set one up at relatively low cost, the disruption of Brexit will most severely be felt by smaller and medium-sized financial institutions, for which the costs of adjusting will be grave. A report by the Boston Consulting Group estimates that a requirement to set up a subsidiary in the EU27 would increase investment banks' global costs by 3 % to 8 %, depending on their current operational model.[26] Private solutions are clearly the second-best solution only.

4. Conclusion

Brexit will inevitably come, but more in form than in substance. The economic case for a financial services deal is strong, political pressure is building up, and the legal framework is remarkably flexible and accommodating. That is, in a nutshell, the central message of my work on the future of European financial integration and the UK.[27] The present contribution has highlighted the different alternatives of negotiating such an agreement.

---

[23] For example, in the AIFMD.

[24] Donal Griffin and Oliver Suess, 'Thiam Says Passport Loss Risks 20 % of His Bank's U.K. Volume' *Bloomberg* (28 September 2016) <https://www.bloomberg.com/news/articles/2016-09-28/credit-suisse-ceo-says-no-passporting-risks-20-of-london-volume> accessed 13 June 2017.

[25] Martin Arnold, 'StanChart picks Frankfurt for EU subsidiary after Brexit' *Financial Times* (3 May 2017) <https://www.ft.com/content/8799a0d4-2ff1-11e7-9555-23ef563ec-f9 a?mhq5j=e3> accessed 13 June 2017.

[26] Philippe Morel, Charles Teschner, Duncan Martin, Will Rhode, and Andreas Bohn, *Global Capital Markets 2016: The Value Migration (Part 2) — Assessing the Impact of Brexit* (BCG White Paper 2016) <http://image-src.bcg.com/BCG-Impact-of-Brexit-on-Capital-Markets-July-2016_tcm9-38972.pdf> accessed 13 June 2017.

[27] See Ringe (n 1).

Three likely outcomes of the negotiating process are (1) Single Market access (2) regulatory equivalence and third-country passport, and (3) private ordering solutions. These three alternatives are by no means exhaustive, and other solutions are conceivable. The negotiation process will inevitably require skill and tactics. Knowing about the options and their implications is winning half the battle.

Wolf-Georg Ringe is a Professor for Law and Economics at the University of Hamburg and a Visiting Professor at the University of Oxford, Faculty of Law.

Brexit and Corporate Governance:
An Economics Perspective

Colin Mayer

To date, the response of the United Kingdom ('UK') economy to the threat of Brexit has been quite benign. As this article is being written, there are gathering clouds in terms of consumer demand and industrial production, but thus far there has not been a pronounced aggregate effect.

One explanation is that the terms of Brexit are yet to be determined. Another is that there has been a compensatory change in the exchange rate that is offsetting the anticipated effects of Brexit. The imposition of trade barriers, the reintroduction of non-trade barriers outside of a single market, and the withdrawal from the customs union impose costs of cross-border activity. These can be offset by depreciation of the exchange rate. Indeed, since the balance of payments must balance, that is precisely what must happen in the presence of a floating rate, and it is what has happened since the referendum in the form of a 20 % depreciation in sterling.

Of course, there is a risk that a depreciation in the exchange rate will not be reflected in a fall in the real exchange rate because of rising wages and inflation. In addition, the depreciation of the exchange rate has very real effects on citizens' standards of living. To the extent that we consume internationally priced goods, we are all 20 % worse off. But from the point of the view of the corporate sector, in aggregate, the price and non-price effects of Brexit can be compensated by price adjustments through the exchange rate.

This is a useful benchmark against which to evaluate Brexit, not least because it provides an explanation for the observation that not much has happened in the first year since the referendum. However, it masks the much more substantial impact that Brexit has on the composition, rather than the aggregate level of activity, and it is to this that we now turn.

1. Who Bears the Brunt of Brexit?

Consider the impact of Brexit on the three factors of production – capital, labour, and land. We know from economic theory that the incidence of an exchange rate adjustment is borne most heavily by the least mobile factor of production. As the least mobile factor, land is most exposed to the depreciation in sterling and, to the extent that prices to date have remained quite static, land has devalued by 20 % in foreign currency terms.

Capital is the most mobile factor and those financial assets that are not invested in domestic physical assets have appreciated by around 20 % or more in domestic currency terms and remained approximately unchanged in foreign currency terms. An illustration of this is the way in which the Financial Times Stock Exchange 100 Index (the 'FTSE 100 Index') has moved almost exactly in inverse relation to the strength of sterling over the past year.

So those productive activities that are intensive in land have, in many cases, become more competitive, whereas those that are dependent on capital have become less competitive as the prospect of increased price and non-price trade barriers has not been offset by reductions in primary factor costs.

Regarding labour, in the absence of offsetting wage rises, labour costs have fallen in foreign currency terms and sectors that are intensive in labour inputs have benefited. However, that is only true of internationally immobile labour. Where firms are competing in international markets for labour, then their real wage costs have not declined.

So firms that are intensive in property and domestic labour have fared the best. Those that are intensive in capital and international pools of labour have fared the worst. To take two examples, the financial sector has fared worst where it is virtual and dependent on high skilled international labour, for example 'fintech', and best where it is branch based and dependent on domestic pools of labour, for example commercial banking. As a second example, higher education has fared well where it is not dependent on international academics and is intensive in the use of domestic property, but poorly where it employs a large pool of internationally mobile academics.

The purpose of this discussion is not so much to undertake an analysis of the winners and losers from Brexit, but to emphasize that there are marked cross-sectional variations in its impact on the corporate sector. This is before one considers the compounding effects of the geographical concentration of some activities in Europe and elsewhere, and the terms of agreements that might be negotiated within the European Union ('EU') and with the rest of the world.

In essence, what is happening is the reverse of the Dutch disease in the 1980 s caused by the appreciation of sterling in response to the emergence of North Sea oil and gas. This had the effect of deindustrializing Britain and it was an important contributor to the explosion of the service sector, including financial services, in the UK. It would have been a mistake to stop the changes that occurred then and it would be a mistake to do so now. So it will be damaging to resist the changes that will occur in financial services and higher education to name the two mentioned before.

Just as we had to let much of industry go in the 1980s, so we will have to let some of our non-industry go in the 2010s and 2020s. Change is painful, but no change is terminal. What should be done is to plan for the changes, direct policy towards facilitating them and ameliorate their most serious social and personal consequences through, for example, well-structured programmes of education and training. There are serious market failures that arise during periods of transition that the public sector can help to alleviate.

2. The role of corporate governance

It is not just the public sector that should help to reduce the costs of the required restructuring; so should the private sector. Change will require corporate governance arrangements capable of managing it. It is no coincidence that one of the first policy statements that Theresa May made as Prime Minister was to exhort a shift in the governance of UK companies – ironically just as we are exiting Europe, in a direction associated with Continental European corporate governance.

A much-debated issue is the extent to which UK corporate law is conducive to the promotion of different types of activities and restructuring of companies.[1] In particular, there is a concern that its emphasis on shareholder interests in Section 172 of the 2006 Companies Act discourages firms from adopting different types of governance arrangements. For example, the presence of workers on company boards to which Theresa May referred in her discussion of corporate governance does not appear to sit comfortably alongside a requirement on directors of companies to act primarily in the interests of their shareholders.

However, the recent UK government consultation on corporate governance in the UK[2] has brought out the fact that, at least in principle, it is possible for companies to take account of other parties and, indeed, according to Section 172, directors are supposed to have regard for the interests of other stakeholders and the long-term success of the company. In addition, the Act allows companies to have altruistic purposes that go beyond the benefit of their shareholders.

So, on the surface, the Companies Act looks quite flexible in allowing companies to adopt different governance structures, and it is suggested that some headway could be made by just requiring companies to report how they have discharged their duties under the Act, including those owed to their other stakeholder interests. In other words, the Companies Act appears to be enabling in allowing companies to adopt appropriate governance arrangements.

There are, though, two fundamental concerns with this interpretation of UK company law. The first is that, notwithstanding the flexibility it grants companies, in practice convention means that companies observe their primary duties to their shareholders and ignore their subsidiary responsibilities to other stakeholders. The second concern is that, irrespective of whether

---

[1] For more extensive discussions of this see Big Innovation Centre, 'The Purposeful Company Interim Report' (London, 2016) and Colin Mayer, 'Who's Responsible for Irresponsible Business?' (2017) 33 (2) Oxf Rev Econ Policy 157–175.

[2] Department for Business, Energy & Industrial Strategy, 'Corporate Governance Reform – Green Paper' (2016). <https://www.gov.uk/government/uploads/system/uploads/attachment_data/file/584013/corporate-governance-reform-green-paper.pdf> accessed 11 June 2017.

the Act is placing sufficient emphasis on stakeholder interests, it is not prioritizing what should be the driver of corporate governance – and that is the company's purpose.

It is potentially erroneous to regard either shareholder or stakeholder interests as primary considerations as against both being derivative of corporate purpose. In other words, the structure of companies in terms of prioritizing the interests of different parties to the firm should be a product of the objective of the company and help in the delivery of it.

This is of particular significance when the nature and purpose of the company may need to undergo change in response to an external influence such as Brexit and alterations in the relative prices of the factors of production. The ability of companies to be able to respond to this by adjusting their purpose and their associated governance arrangements may be of critical significance in promoting a smooth transition to the new state of the economy.

The adoption of alternative model companies within the framework of the Companies Act might be one way in which this could be achieved. Companies could adopt public benefit, stakeholder participation, or privileged shareholder arrangements that allow them to specify a public benefit over and above their financial returns, their accountability to different stakeholder groups, and the privileging of certain classes of shareholders.[3] By specifying these alternative arrangements, greater substance could be given to the flexibility that is in principle, but not currently, in practice associated with UK company law.

In summary, the marked changes in the composition of the UK economy that are in prospect as a consequence of Brexit will require company law and corporate governance systems that are sufficiently enabling and flexible to respond appropriately to the changing circumstances and needs of companies.

Colin Mayer is Peter Moores Professor of Management
Studies at Saïd Business School, University of Oxford.

---

[3] Big Innovation Centre, 'The Purposeful Company Policy Report' (London, February 2017) <http://www.biginnovationcentre.com/media/uploads/pdf/TPC_InterimExecutiveRemunerationReport.pdf> accessed 11 June 2017.

The Brexit Stakes for Corporate Activity – a Restructuring & Insolvency Perspective

Wolfram Prusko

The United Kingdom ('UK') provides an important legal and financial infrastructure for corporate activity in Europe. With respect to the type of corporate activity that may be impacted by a 'hard Brexit,' financial restructuring and corporate insolvency are very prominent topics that should be – and actually are very actively – addressed. As a major hub for financial activities, corporates all over Europe turn regularly to England when their finances are concerned.[1] This preference includes companies in distress that seek to restructure their financial liabilities and to compromise with their creditors – either within or outside of formal insolvency processes. In short: London currently is beyond doubt, and not without reason, the centre for financial restructurings in Europe: so what is at stake with Brexit?

In my opinion, any discussions regarding Brexit's impact on restructuring and insolvency must address three major aspects:

First, with 'hard Brexit' it will be difficult – if achievable at all in a reasonably near future – to have an integrated cross-border conflicts regime for formal insolvency proceedings that is comparable to the current *status quo*.

Second, the practical impact of such procedural disintegration on financial restructurings may be limited if the UK succeeds in maintaining a certain level of recognition for the Scheme of Arrangement, arguably its most successful and well-known out-of-court restructuring tool.

Third, if English law remains the preferred jurisdiction for banking and finance contracts, contractual work-out arrangements typically included in standard inter-creditor agreements can be expected to adapt quickly to the changed circumstances and provide for practical work-arounds on most issues.

---

[1] According to Bloomberg, London courts restructured more than $5 bn of foreign company debt in 2015, with Spanish and German companies leading the table for debt restructured in the UK between 2009 and 2015 (see Luca Casiraghi and Jeremy Hodges, 'London Lure for Troubled Firms Threatened by Spanish Gamble' *Bloomberg Law* (15 November 2015) <https://bol.bna.com/london-lure-for-troubled-firms-threatened-by-spanish-gamble/> accessed 6 June 2017).

1. The expected procedural disintegration

The current insolvency framework within the European Union ('EU') is primarily governed by its Insolvency Regulation ('EIR').[2] Given that this regulation is largely a conflicts-of-law regime, it determines the applicable law, the competent courts, and the automatic EU-wide recognition of court actions. Initial weaknesses and drawbacks inherent in the regulation recently have been addressed in its recast version for proceedings starting halfway through this year. The regulation also has been expanded to govern cross-border insolvencies of corporate groups by means of coordination rules.[3] Once Brexit occurs, with the EIR ceasing to be applicable to the UK, neither the opening of English insolvency proceedings, nor court decisions rendered therein will automatically and consistently be recognised throughout the EU.[4] Instead, the national regimes of the remaining Member States will have authority to make determinations and issue decisions on recognition of English decisions case by case.[5]

The result likely will be a fragmented situation that potentially will deter, or significantly increase, transaction costs for COMI shifts, or other structures using English insolvency proceedings for pan-European cross-border matters. Any such result potentially may be capable of being mitigated by, eg, treaty accession to the EIR. However – unlike the Lugano Convention for the civil forum with European Free Trade Association ('EFTA') States[6] – to date, this has not been tested outside EU membership. Thus, there is a fair chance that the procedural disintegration for insolvency proceedings cannot be effectively addressed within the near future, unless focused upon as a matter within the Brexit negotiations.

2. The competitive challenge for out-of-court restructurings

The tool that has most prominently shaped the European restructuring landscape is the English Scheme of Arrangement. Situated in the English Companies Act[7] rather than in England's insolvency laws, a wide array of

---

[2] Council Regulation (EC) 1346/2000 of 29 May 2000 on insolvency proceedings [2000] OJ L 160/1, as well as the recast Council Regulation (EU) 2015/848 of 20 May 2015 on insolvency proceedings [2015] OJ L 141/19, applicable from 26 June 2017 ('EIR (2015)'), including in the UK (Recital 87 of EIR (2015)). This article does not address special sector rules applicable to, eg, financial institutions, which are exempt from the application of the EIR.

[3] See new Chapter V EIR (2015).

[4] Unlike under Chapter II EIR.

[5] Recognition, eg, upon application as proposed by Art 15ff of the UNCITRAL Model Law on Cross-Border Insolvency (1997), or as automatic recognition (eg, under § 343 of the German Insolvency Code).

[6] Convention on jurisdiction and the recognition and enforcement of judgments in civil and commercial matters of 30 October 2007 [2007] OJ L 339/3 ('Lugano Convention').

[7] Part 26 (sections 895–901) of the Companies Act 2006.

applications was developed during the last years for restructuring debt of companies domiciled all over Europe (and beyond).[8] Its success, in my view, is based on a unique combination of English law as the preeminent jurisdiction for finance contracts and the common perception of predictable and commercially savvy courts.

Interestingly, under the current EU framework, recognition of these schemes is not achieved under the EIR.[9] Instead, the UK Scheme of Arrangement's recognition is based on (i) its validity as a contractual arrangement under private international law following English choice of law and (ii) the recognition of the civil court decisions sanctioning these schemes with reference to the Brussels I Regulation.[10]

The recognition test under private international law should remain unchanged after Brexit, as the Rome I Regulation continues to determine the test for the application of English law in the remaining Member States.[11] Without the Brussels I Regulation, and in the absence of international treaties,[12] however, recognising the English Scheme of Arrangement as a civil court decision will be up to the laws and courts of the Member State concerned.

An aspect that may create a more challenging environment is the EU Commission's recently established agenda to develop and harmonise the out-of-court restructuring regimes in the Member States in the interest of the common capital market. A draft directive was issued in November 2016.[13] It is doubtful whether this agenda will be fully completed and effective by the time the UK formally leaves the EU. English courts applying the UK Scheme of Arrangement will thus continue to be in an advantageous position, in particular if the current level of recognition under the applicable civil procedure regime can be maintained, for example by the UK's accession to the Lugano Convention.[14] If this is not the case, continental competitors such

---

[8] See, eg, more recent cases such as *CBR Fashion GmbH* [2016] EWHC 2808 (Ch); *DTEK Finance PLC* sanctioned by court order dated 21 December 2016; *Global Garden Products* [2016] EWHC 1884 (Ch); *Van Gansewinkel Groep BV* [2015] EWHC 2151 (Ch).

[9] These schemes are not included in the EIR's Annex A, which contains a comprehensive list of all proceedings to which the EIR applies (see Art 1 EIR).

[10] Council Regulation (EU) 1215/2012 of 12 December 2012 on jurisdiction and the recognition and enforcement of judgments in civil and commercial matters (recast) [2012] OJ 351/1.

[11] See Art 2 of Council Regulation (EC) No 593/2008 of 17 June 2008 on the law applicable to contractual obligations (Rome I) [2008] OJ L 177/6.

[12] For potential relevant options, see Giesela Rühl, 'The Effect of Brexit on the Resolution of International Disputes – Choice of Law and Jurisdiction in Civil and Commercial Matters' (*Oxford Business Law Blog*, 13 April 2017) <https://www.law.ox.ac.uk/business-law-blog/blog/2017/04/brexit-negotiations-series-'-effect-brexit-resolution-international> accessed 6 June 2017.

[13] European Commission, 'Proposal for a directive of the European Parliament and of the Council on preventive restructuring frameworks, second chance and measures to increase the efficiency of restructuring, insolvency and discharge procedures and amending Directive 2012/30/EU' COM(2016) 723 final.

[14] Art 33 of the Lugano Convention provides for the recognition of court decisions issued by another contracting state's court.

as Germany, Italy, or the Netherlands may try to step up and to wrest restructuring cases away from England with their own enhanced and EU-wide recognised restructuring processes.[15]

3. Market adaptation

Relying on general freedom of contracts rather than on a special statutory restructuring framework, the financial community has developed a very elaborate contractual regime for restructuring companies in distress, which in Europe regularly is governed by English law. Such arrangements are typically included in inter-creditor agreements between the various lenders and lender groups, and address the usual issues of financial restructuring on a contractual basis: waterfall distribution to give effect to priority ranking, majority creditor decisions for efficiently re-capitalising the debtor's assets, debt relief, and release of collateral and guarantees, to name only a few.[16] We expect parties in the financing markets to continue to make use of such contractual arrangements in connection with and in contemplation of financial restructurings; whether or not English courts, which already have a track record in ruling on disputes thereunder, remain the preferred forums may mostly be driven by whether or not English law in general remains the preeminent jurisdiction for finance contracts. Given the flexibility of financial contracting, one would expect that any practical roadblocks preventing full effect of such arrangements after Brexit will be resolved in a rapid, evolutionary manner – which can happen in real time over the Brexit negotiation as results become apparent even before the effective date of Brexit.

Wolfram Prusko is Partner
at Kirkland & Ellis, Munich.[17]

---

[15] In particular, the Netherlands has been discussing the introduction of a tool similar to the English scheme of arrangement since 2014 (*Wet continuïteit ondernemingen II*).

[16] See Leo Plank and Wolfram Prusko, 'Die Intercreditor Vereinbarung als Instrument der internationalen Restrukturierung' in Hommel, Knecht and Wohlenberg (eds) *Handbuch Unternehmensrestrukturierung* (2nd ed, forthcoming).

[17] This contribution reflects the personal opinion of the author and is not and cannot be attributed to Kirkland & Ellis; it was presented on the conference 'Negotiating Brexit' held in Oxford on 17 March 2017, the forum of which also determined the format of the text.

The Effect of Brexit on the Resolution of International Disputes: Choice of Law and Jurisdiction in Civil and Commercial Matters

Giesela Rühl

Over the last decades, England has become a prime, if not the prime centre for settling international disputes: international companies choose English law more often than any other law as governing law. And they choose to settle their disputes more often before English courts than before other courts. The question of how Brexit will affect the legal framework for the resolution of international disputes is, therefore, of quite some importance – both for United Kingdom ('UK') and European Union ('EU') companies. This contribution explores the ramifications of Brexit for choice of law and jurisdiction in civil and commercial matters and makes suggestions for the future legal framework, taking into account the UK government's two recent Brexit White Papers of 2 February and 30 March 2017.[1]

1. Current legal framework

Choice of law and jurisdiction is currently regulated by three EU Regulations. The law applicable to contractual and non-contractual obligations is determined with the help of the Rome I Regulation[2] and the Rome II Regulation.[3] Jurisdiction is governed by the Brussels Ia Regulation.[4] All three regulations apply throughout the EU (with the exception of Denmark), and there is broad agreement that they establish a fairly clear and predictable legal framework for the settlement of international disputes, especially because choice of law and choice of forum clauses will be enforced under the same conditions across the EU.

---

[1] Department for Exiting the European Union, 'The United Kingdom's exit from and new partnership with the European Union. White Paper' (2017) <https://www.gov.uk/government/publications/the-united-kingdoms-exit-from-and-new-partnership-with-the-european-union-white-paper#history> accessed 21 May 2017; Department for Exiting the European Union, 'Legislating for the United Kingdom's Withdrawal from the European Union. White Paper' (2017) <https://www.gov.uk/government/uploads/system/uploads/attachment_data/file/604516/Great_repeal_bill_white_paper_accessible.pdf> accessed 21 May 2017.

[2] European Parliament and Council Regulation (EC) 593/2008 of 17 June on the law applicable to contractual obligations (Rome I), [2008] OJ L 177/6.

[3] European Parliament and Council Regulation (EC) 864/2007 of 11 July on the law applicable to non-contractual obligations (Rome II), [2007] OJ L 199/40.

[4] European Parliament and Council Regulation (EU) 1215/2012 of 12 December on jurisdiction and the recognition and enforcement of judgments in civil and commercial matters (recast), [2012] OJ L 351/1.

2. Future legal framework: Baseline ('Hard Brexit')

Now, what happens if the UK leaves the EU? Of course, the above-mentioned regulations will cease to apply. But which provisions will take their place? The details are disputed and a full discussion is beyond the scope of this contribution.[5] Suffice it to say that I do not think that the Rome Convention on the law applicable to contractual obligations of 1980 or the Brussels Conventions on jurisdiction, recognition, and enforcement of judgments of 1968 may become effective and applicable again after Brexit.[6] UK courts will, therefore, have to resort to their national (statutory or common) law to determine the applicable law and to determine jurisdiction once the Rome I, the Rome II, and the Brussels Ia Regulations cease to have effect. Courts in the remaining Member States, by contrast, will continue to apply the Rome I and II Regulations. And they will also continue to apply the Brussels Ia Regulation to the extent that it applies to third states. To the extent that the Brussels Ia Regulation does not cover third state cases, Member State courts will apply their own national rules to determine jurisdiction. In particular, they will apply their own national rules of jurisdiction to determine the validity of a choice of forum clause in favour of English courts.

As a consequence, choice of law and jurisdiction will no longer be subject to the same regime in the UK and the rest of the EU once Brexit becomes effective. This will make it harder for parties to predict which law will apply to international disputes and which court will be competent to hear a case. The worst thing, however, is that parties cannot trust anymore that choice of law and choice of forum clauses will be equally enforced in the UK and the remaining Member States.[7] Since different legal regimes will apply, the enforceability of such clauses will essentially depend on where a lawsuit will eventually be brought.

---

[5] See, however, for a detailed account, Richard Aikens and Andrew Dinsmore, 'Jurisdiction, Enforcement and the Conflict of Laws in Cross-Border commercial Disputes: What Are the Legal Consequences of Brexit?' (2016) 27 EBLR 903 ff; Guillaume Croisant, 'Fog in Channel – Continent Cut Off. Les conséquences juridiques du Brexit pour le droit international privé et l'arbitrage international' (2017) JT 24 ff; Andrew Dickinson, 'Back to the future: The UK's EU exit and the conflict of laws' (2016) J Priv Int'l L 195 ff; Burkhard Hess 'Back to the Past: BREXIT und das europäische internationale Privat- und Verfahrensrecht' (2016) IPRax 409 ff; Eva Lein, 'Unchartered Territory? A few Thoughts on Private International Law post Brexit' (2015) 17 YbPIL 33 ff; Sara Masters and Belinda McRae, 'What Does Brexit Mean for the Brussels Regime?' (2016) J Int'l Arb 483 ff; Giesela Rühl, 'Die Wahl englischen Rechts und englischer Gerichte. Zur Zukunft des Justizstandortes England' (2017) JZ 72 ff; Johannes Ungerer, 'Brexit von Brüssel und den anderen Verordnungen zum Internationalen Privat- und Verfahrensrecht' in M Kramme, Chr. Baldus and M. Schmidt-Kessel (eds), *Brexit und die Juristischen Folgen* (Nomos, Baden-Baden 2017) 296 ff.

[6] See, for a detailed discussion, Rühl (n5) 74, 77.

[7] See, for a detailed discussion, Rühl (n5) 76, 79.

3. Future Legal Framework: 'Soft Brexit' scenario

What are the alternatives to the just described 'hard Brexit' scenario? I think that one may consider essentially four options. These will be presented as four separate alternatives. However, they are not necessarily mutually exclusive.

a) 1ˢᵗ Option: agreement on continued application of EU framework

The first – and most straightforward – option would certainly be to aim for an agreement between the UK and the EU that the Rome I, the Rome II, and the Brussels Ia Regulations will continue to apply even after Brexit.[8] This might look counter-intuitive at first sight, but the idea of the 'Great Repeal Bill' proves that the UK government has the intention to keep at least some European rules post-Brexit. And since judicial cooperation was not on the agenda of the Brexiteers, preserving the *status quo* as regards choice of law and jurisdiction would probably not do much political harm.

The problem with the continued application of the current framework is, of course, that it requires the EU's consent. And the EU might withhold that very consent for various reasons, notably for the purpose of setting an example vis-à-vis other Member States that toy with the idea of leaving the EU.[9] In addition, the EU's consent to continue applying the existing EU instruments will almost certainly depend on the UK accepting the jurisprudence of the Court of Justice of the European Union ('CJEU') in one form or the other. However, it was – and still is – one of the central aims of Brexit and the UK government 'to bring an end to the jurisdiction of the CJEU in the UK'.[10] So, one would have to find a new arrangement to ensure uniform application and interpretation. One potential model is the mechanism enshrined in Protocol No 2 to the Lugano Convention of 2007,[11] which requires the courts of non-Member States to 'pay due account' to CJEU decisions (as well as decisions from other contracting states) and could be an acceptable compromise for both the UK and the EU.

---

[8] Likewise, Aikens and Dinsmore (n5) 914 (as regards the Brussels Ia Regulation); Lein (n5) 41; Masters and McRae (n5) 484 (as regards the Brussels Ia Regulation); Ungerer (n5) 307. See also the Report of the Justice Committee of the House of Commons, 'Implications of Brexit for the justice system' (Ninth Report of Session 2016–2017, HC 750, 22 March 2017), 16 para 32; as well as the Report of the European Union Committee of the House of Lords, 'Brexit: Justice for families, individuals and businesses?' (17ᵗʰ Report of Session 2016–2017, HL Paper 134, 20 March 2017) 11 para 23 and 42 para 1.

[9] Croisant (n5) 28; Masters and McRae (n5) 486. See also Lein (n5) 41.

[10] Department for Exiting the European Union (n1) 13.

[11] Aikens and Dinsmore (n8) 915. See also the Report of the European Union Committee of the House of Lords (n8) 39 para 127, 44 para 23, as well as the Report of the Justice Committee of the House of Commons (n8) 3, 18 para 35, 24 para 5.

b) 2nd Option: negotiation of a new Treaty with the EU

The second option is as straightforward as the first, even though more difficult to implement. It consists of negotiating a new treaty with the EU on issues of choice of law and jurisdiction and, of course, recognition and enforcement. This option probably comes closest to what the UK government has in mind when it speaks of a 'new strategic partnership with the EU'[12] and the aim of building a new relationship with the help of a new Trade Agreement. It would also allow the UK to improve the current legal framework where it is perceived to be deficient from a UK perspective. For example, it might try to renegotiate the current European position shaped by various European Court of Justice judgments as regards the doctrine of *forum non conveniens* and as regards the use of anti-suit injunctions.

However, the negotiation of a 'new deal' will be time-consuming. Considering how many years it took to negotiate the existing EU instruments, and considering that judicial cooperation will not be the top priority during the upcoming negotiations, it is unlikely that a new 'deal' could be signed and enter into force on the day of Brexit. Also, the UK and the EU would have to find a way to deal with and settle disputes arising under the new regime. The UK government suggests that one could think of creating a new settlement mechanism along the lines of other international agreements, such as the General Agreement on Tariffs and Trade ('GATT'), the North American Free Trade Agreement ('NAFTA'), or the EU-Canada Comprehensive Economic and Trade Agreement ('CETA').[13] Yet, it is rather unclear whether the EU would be willing to build a new court system alongside the CJEU to deal with issues of choice of law and jurisdiction.

c) 3rd Option: unilateral application of EU instruments

The third option becomes attractive if the first two options fail. In this case, the UK could simply decide to apply the Rome I, the Rome II, and the Brussels Ia Regulations unilaterally. This is in line with the UK government's idea of a 'Great Repeal Bill', which is supposed 'to convert...the body of existing EU law...into domestic law'.[14] However, the problem with this option is that it does not work for jurisdiction (and, I may add, it does not work at all for recognition and enforcement of judgements):[15] the Brussels Ia Regulation is a measure of international civil procedure and, therefore, rests on the principle of reciprocity.

---

[12] Department for Exiting the European Union (n1) 35.

[13] Department for Exiting the European Union (n1) 9. See for the details Department for Exiting the European Union (n1).

[14] Department for Exiting the European Union (n1) 9. See for the details Department for Exiting the European Union (n1).

[15] Ungerer (n8) 306. See also the Report of the European Union Committee of the House of Lords (n8) 21 para 56, 42 para 8, as well as the Report of the Justice Committee of the House of Commons (n8) 115 para 28.

Unilateral application, however, works well as regards choice of law.[16] And since the 'Great Repeal Bill' will most likely require UK courts to give '*historic* CJEU case law...the same binding, or precedent status as decisions of the UK Supreme Court',[17] unilateral application of the Rome I and II Regulations will go a long way to preserve the *status quo*. The problem that remains, though, is that unilateral application of both Regulations can ensure long term uniform application only if the UK courts are also required to follow or give 'due account' to *future* CJEU decisions. Should they not be so required, the third option will remain incomplete and only create the illusion of uniformity in the long run.

d) 4th Option: negotiation and adoption of international treaties

This brings me to the fourth option: The UK could replace the current European regime with a more global regime by negotiating new treaties with non-EU countries, for example in the framework of the Hague Conference on Private International Law. This, however, will take time and, therefore, is no short-term solution. A short-term solution, however, would be to sign existing international treaties such as the Lugano Convention of 2007 and the Hague Convention on Choice of Court Agreements of 2005.[18] This would help to avoid at least some of the negative effects described earlier. However, it would not go all the way to preserve the benefits of the *status quo*: the Lugano Convention of 2007 has not (yet) been aligned with the Brussels Ia Regulation. The substantial improvements that the recast has brought about, some of which were introduced because the UK lobbied hard for them, would, therefore, not extend to the UK. The Hague Choice of Court Convention, for its part, covers only choice of forum clauses and does not deal with other grounds of jurisdiction – and it only covers certain choice of forum clauses. Finally, the Convention is by no means – at least not yet – the global Convention it was meant to be. In fact, it is to this day only in force and applicable in the EU (with the exception of Denmark), Mexico, and Singapore.[19]

---

[16] Aikens and Dinsmore (n8) 917; Croisant (n5) 31; Dickinson (n5) 210; Lein (n8) 42. See also the recommendations of the European Union Committee of the House of Lords (n8) 38 para 125, 44 para 22 and of the Justice Committee of the House of Commons (n8) 115 para 28, 16 paras 32, 24 para 4.

[17] Department for Exiting the European Union (n1) 14, 15, paras 2.14–2.17.

[18] Aikens and Dinsmore (n8) 912, 915; Dickinson (n5) 209; Lein (n5) 39, 40; Masters and McRae (n5) 487, 494; Ungerer (n5) 302, 303. See also the recommendations of the European Union Committee of the House of Lords (n8) 36 para 117, 44 para 22, and of the Justice Committee of the House of Commons, (n8) 15 para 28, 16 para 32, 24 para 4.

[19] See the status chart available at <https://www.hcch.net/en/instruments/conventions/status-table/?cid=98> accessed 21 May 2017.

4. Conclusions

The preceding analysis shows that there is no easy and no perfect way out of the problems Brexit will create. The best short-term option for both the UK and the EU would probably be to agree on the continued application of the existing EU instruments within the framework of the withdrawal agreement, or in a separate agreement. If this turns out to be not possible, the second-best short-term option for the UK will be to apply the Rome I and Rome II Regulations unilaterally, and to sign the Lugano Convention of 2007 and the Hague Convention on Choice of Court Agreements. In the medium and long-term, the UK is probably well advised to apply a global strategy and to foster the conclusion of more international treaties in the framework of the Hague Conference on Private International Law.

Giesela Rühl is Professor of Civil Law, Civil Procedure,
Private International Law, International Civil
Procedure, European Private Law and Comparative
Law at the Friedrich Schiller University of Jena
(Germany).

Negotiating Brexit:
Recognition and Enforcement of Judgments[1]

Tom Snelling

Although it could never attract as many tabloid headlines as other 'negotiating Brexit' issues, a successful resolution to questions about the future framework for recognition and enforcement of judgments is key for safeguarding individuals' rights and the success of any United Kingdom ('UK')-European Union ('EU') trading relations post-Brexit.

The UK has publicly acknowledged that the regime established by the recast Brussels Regulation ('Brussels Recast') incorporates 'important principles that will form part of the negotiations';[2] however, it is uncertain how high up the UK's priority list for the negotiations this issue will feature and how it will be covered in any agreement reached.

This is not just a concern for those going into bat for the UK in the Brexit negotiations: the EU27 Member States will also want to ensure that judgments of their courts can be enforced effectively in the UK. The EU's current Brexit negotiating guidelines also make clear that the agreement governing the UK's withdrawal 'should ensure that the recognition and execution of national judicial decisions handed down before the withdrawal date remain governed by the relevant provisions of Union law…'.[3] The position of post-Brexit judgments is more uncertain.

This article discusses the current state of play, the possible outcomes if the UK and EU27 do not take any pro-active steps in this regard, and the alternative options available for a long-term arrangement. As with other Brexit-related issues, this is expected to be a complex part of the negotiations. As other practitioners have noted, dealing with this out of the political spotlight will best 'enable cool heads to reach agreement on these technical points'.[4]

---

[1] With thanks to Lauma Skruzmane, Ashmita Garrett, Ramya Arnold and Phoebe Chan, also within the Dispute Resolution team at Freshfields Bruckhaus Deringer LLP.

[2] Oliver Heald QC, MP, 'Corrected oral evidence: Brexit: civil justice co-operation and the CJEU' (*the European Union Justice Sub-Committee of the House of Lords*, 31 January 2017) Q38 <http://data.parliament.uk/writtenevidence/committeeevidence.svc/evidencedocument/eu-justice-subcommittee/brexit-civil-justice-cooperation/oral/46539.html> accessed 31 May 2017.

[3] Council, 'Annex: Directives for the negotiation of an agreement with the United Kingdom of Great Britain and Northern Ireland setting out the arrangements for its withdrawal from the European Union' (2017) 210009/17 BXT 16 ADD 1 <https://ec.europa.eu/commission/publications/negotiating-directives-article-50-negotiations_en> accessed 31 May 2017.

[4] Stuart Pickford and Mark Stefanini, 'Brexit negotiations must make cross-border contract disputes clear cut' (*The Sunday Times*, 25 May 2017) <http://www.thetimes.co.uk/article/1a612162-4096-11e7-9319-8b08a5454daf> accessed 31 May 2017.

1. Current regime

Under Article 42(1) of Brussels Recast, a party who is the beneficiary of a judgment delivered in one EU Member State and wishes to enforce it in another simply needs to provide the competent enforcement authority in that other Member State with a certificate issued by the court that has delivered the judgment and a copy of the judgment which satisfies the conditions necessary to establish its authenticity.

Brussels Recast has sought to set a high bar for refusal of recognition and enforcement. Consequently, under the current regime, a party dealing with a counterparty elsewhere in the EU can be reasonably confident of being able to enforce a judgment delivered in one Member State against a counterparty in another.

As so often in life, practical reality proves more complex than theory. Parties have experienced obstacles to the free movement of judgments across the EU under Brussels Recast. In particular, the public policy exception under Article 45 can be (and has been) interpreted widely by Member State courts. This can ultimately result in the recognition and enforcement of judgments being subject to national law by the backdoor, with proceedings becoming drawn out where there are several tiers of appeal in that jurisdiction.

2. Default position post-Brexit

a) Recognition and enforcement of EU27 court judgments by UK courts

If the UK Government elects to do nothing, Brussels Recast will no longer apply in relation to the recognition and enforcement of EU27 court judgments after Brexit. Consequently, the courts of England and Wales will most likely have to resort to common law rules.[5] While circumstances in which the recognition and enforcement of EU27 judgments would fail to satisfy the common law requirements are likely to be limited, ultimately, the enforcement process may become more cumbersome and time-consuming post-Brexit.

The prospects of IndyRef2, let alone a referendum which reaches an outcome different to that of 18 September 2014, may be receding. That said, Brexit also raises the awkward question of what would happen in terms of judgment recognition between an independent Scotland, the remaining legal jurisdictions of the UK, and the EU27.

b) Recognition and enforcement of UK judgments by the courts in the EU27

The position will be similar in the EU27 post-Brexit. Enforcement of UK judgments (which post-Brexit will be third state court judgments) across the

---

[5] *See Adams v Cape Industries plc* [1990] Ch 433 on the enforcement of judgments at common law which also summarises the key requirements.

EU27 will be subject to the national laws of each Member State. However, the national laws on recognition of third state court judgments vary and indeed, in a number of jurisdictions, the procedure is more cumbersome than the automatic recognition rules under Brussels Recast.

Ultimately, the Brussels Recast regime is (at least) a two-way street, and the EU27 Member States also have a vested interest in finding a workable solution to protecting judgment creditors, who post-Brexit will be seeking to enforce a domestic judgment from courts in the EU27 against assets in the UK.

3. Other options

The other possible options for the UK include:

(1) entering into a bespoke UK-EU agreement on the continued application of Brussels Recast (or a framework to that effect);

(2) acceding to the 2007 Lugano Convention ('Lugano') as an independent party; and

(3) acceding to the 2005 Hague Convention ('Hague') as an independent party.

a) Bespoke UK-EU Agreement

To preserve the *status quo*, a new treaty would have to be negotiated between the EU and the UK (or provisions included in any overarching withdrawal agreement) providing for reciprocal arrangements for recognition and enforcement of judgments. This is unlikely to be straightforward, as such a bespoke UK-EU treaty would require unanimity among the EU27.

Denmark concluded such a bespoke treaty with the EU since it is not bound by the relevant treaty provisions under which Brussels Recast was enacted. Importantly, however, the Danish agreement provides for references from the courts of Denmark to the Court of Justice of the European Union ('the CJEU') and for CJEU jurisprudence on Brussels Recast to be taken into account by the Danish courts. Denmark also cannot enter into international agreements that affect or alter the scope of Brussels Recast without the EU's consent. Given the current political climate, these aspects of such a bespoke treaty are unlikely to be acceptable to the UK Government. Are there more politically palatable alternative options?

b) Lugano

Lugano, which regulates recognition and enforcement issues, is currently applicable in Switzerland, Norway, and Iceland, as well as in the EU Member States. These rules are a step behind Brussels Recast. Nevertheless, by comparison with doing nothing, acceding to Lugano as an independent party would be a tenable fall-back option for the UK as it would preserve some of the reciprocal benefits of Brussels Recast. Importantly, however, as further discussed below, pursuing this option would require the UK courts to take 'due account' of CJEU jurisprudence.

c) Hague

The UK could also join Hague as an independent party and could do so unilaterally without the consent of the other signatories.

However, the impact of Hague is limited as, currently, only judgments rendered pursuant to exclusive jurisdiction clauses are recognised and enforced. Moreover, like Lugano, Hague does not benefit from the expedited procedure in Brussels Recast. In addition, beyond the EU Member States (except Denmark), only Mexico and Singapore participate in it. The list of contracting states is likely to increase, at least with the addition of the US and Ukraine that have signed, but not yet ratified, it. So, while Hague provides some relief, it is not the final answer.

4. Key issues for those litigating post-Brexit

a) CJEU

The most delicate (and perhaps tempestuous) issue to be resolved in relation to any post-Brexit agreement on the issues of recognition and enforcement is the future role of Luxembourg. The UK has made it clear that it intends to end the jurisdiction of the CJEU and that the courts of England and Wales will not be required to consider the CJEU's jurisprudence made after Brexit.[6]

If any workable post-Brexit solution is unlikely without accepting some form of role for the CJEU, hostility towards the CJEU among many in the UK (fuelled regularly by 'Brexiteering' aspects of the UK media) could be a deal-breaker when it comes to a continuation of any aspects of Brussels Recast – either in the form of a bespoke UK-EU agreement, or under Lugano.

Ultimately, the position on the weight of CJEU jurisprudence may end up being settled in respect of other areas of negotiating Brexit and the same applied to any continuing framework based on Brussels Recast.

b) Courts of England and Wales

Depending on their priorities, the uncertainty with recognition and enforcement of judgments following the UK's departure from the Brussels Recast framework may encourage debate as to when the UK courts (particularly those in England and Wales) are the most appropriate choice of court.

---

[6] Department for Exiting the European Union, 'Legislating for the United Kingdom's Withdrawal from the European Union. White Paper' (London, 2017), 2.13 <https://www.gov.uk/government/uploads/system/uploads/attachment_data/file/604516/Great_repeal_bill_-white_paper_accessible.pdf> accessed 31 May 2017.

Our courts have long been the forum of choice for cross-border litigation in the EU and internationally. Many of the reasons why parties select them are unrelated to Brussels Recast and, therefore, unaffected by Brexit. These include, among other things: the fundamental constitutional principles underpinning the common law system, such as the doctrine of precedent, judicial independence, and the near unrivalled calibre of the judiciary, the availability of specialist courts and specialist judges for technical cases such as the Commercial and Admiralty Court and the Technology and Construction Court, and the availability of high quality dispute resolution practitioners, procedural certainty, speedy procedure for interim injunctions, and availability of a wide range of remedies.

At the same time, it is important to recognise some of the challengers. For example, Singapore has been attracting international parties to its courts by explicitly modelling them on the London Commercial Court. In addition, courts in other major European financial centres such as Paris, Frankfurt, and Amsterdam also now offer capabilities to hear cases in English, or are thinking of making it easier for English law governed cases to be heard in their courts.

5. The way forward

Irrespective of what path the UK will choose to take post-Brexit, in due course, the reality is that there is likely to be uncertainty for quite some time. What steps can parties take to mitigate this?

Parties entering into contracts now should consider whether they are prepared to take a risk on enforcement of judgments in the EU27, even if the process is slower/more complex. Various factors may well tip the balance in favour of continuing to litigate in the courts of England and Wales. In such cases, parties may continue to choose the exclusive jurisdiction clause of the courts of England and Wales.

If parties are sufficiently concerned about enforcement, they could include a 'Brexit trigger clause' (ie, wording to enable parties to arbitrate, or use a dispute resolution forum other than the courts of England and Wales when a dispute arises, if there is no reciprocal post-Brexit arrangement for the enforcement of judgments). Alternatively, a London seated arbitration could be agreed upon upfront.

The path that people choose to tread is likely to depend upon appetite for risk, the nature of the contract to be concluded, and the factual context; for example, is litigation likely, is consensual dispute resolution possible, and where are the parties' assets located?

While this will sound obvious, to ensure maximum protection of their interests, parties should weigh up their options carefully and seek legal advice, as appropriate.

One politician leading the Brexit campaign during last year's referendum famously said that we have 'had enough of experts'.[7] Those trying to work out the impact of Brexit on their litigation strategy choices (let alone those tasked with negotiating Brexit) may find greater comfort in access to wise counsel.

Tom Snelling is litigation partner at
Freshfields Bruckhaus Deringer LLP.

---

[7] Henry Mance, 'Britain has had enough of experts, says Gove' (*Financial Times*, 3 June 2016) <https://www.ft.com/content/3be49734-29cb-11e6-83e4-abc22d5d108c> accessed 31 May 2017.

The Effect of Brexit on the Resolution
of International Disputes: The Impact of Brexit
on International Commercial Arbitration

Marco Torsello

Although new jurisdictions are becoming increasingly attractive as seats for international arbitration,[1] most commentators seem to agree that the role of London as a centre for international commercial arbitration is unlikely to be negatively affected by Brexit.[2] The sources of law governing arbitration (the 1958 New York Convention[3] and the 1996 Arbitration Act[4]) will remain unaffected by Brexit, irrespective of how Brexit will happen.[5] Moreover, the arena of international commercial arbitration is, by its own nature, global and therefore 'immune' from the 'regional' contingencies caused by the discontinuance of the current relationship between the United Kingdom ('UK') and the European Union ('EU'). In fact, the 'arbitration exception' in the Brussels-I Recast[6] ('Recast Regulation') regime (Article 1(2)(d)) confirms the autonomous status of arbitration[7] and its potential 'immunization' from the vicissitudes of the relationships between the remaining EU Member States and the UK.

---

[1] On the emergence of newer seats in arbitration, cf Jan Paulson, Emmanuel Gaillard, David W Rivkin, *Current Issues and Future Challenges in International Arbitration* (IBA Publisher 2015).

[2] Cf, for instance, Mohamed Salahudine Abdel Wahab, 'Brexit's Chilling Effect on Choice of Law and Arbitration in the United Kingdom: Practical Reflections Between Aggravation and Alleviation' (2016) 33 J Int'l Arb 463, arguing that 'the post-Brexit broad availability of anti-suit injunctions in the UK may be seen, in some cases, as an advantage towards choosing London as a seat of arbitration' (at 473), citing in support the CityUK Survey on arbitration (see TheCityUK, 'UK legal services 2016 – Legal Excellence, Internationally Renowned' (2016) <https://www.thecityuk.com/assets/2016/Reports-PDF/UK-Legal-services-2016.pdf> accessed 10 June 2017). *Contra:* see Michael McIlwrath, 'An Unamicable Separation: Brexit Consequences for London as a Premier Seat of International Dispute Resolution in Europe' (2016) 33 J Int'l Arb 451 ff.

[3] Convention on the Recognition and Enforcement of Foreign Arbitral Awards, (New York, 10 June 1958) <http://www.uncitral.org/pdf/english/texts/arbitration/NY-conv/New-York-Convention-E.pdf> accessed 10 June 2017. As of May 2017, this Convention has been ratified, or otherwise adopted, by 157 States.

[4] Arbitration Act (1966, reprinted in 2001) <http://www.legislation.gov.uk/ukpga/1996/23/contents> accessed 10 June 2017.

[5] On how Brexit will happen, see, eg, Holger P Hestemeyer, 'How Brexit Will Happen: A Brief Primer on European Union Law and Constitutional Law Questions Raised by Brexit' (2016) 33 J Int'l Arb 429 ff.

[6] European Parliament and Council Regulation (EU) No 1215/2012 of 12 December 2012 on jurisdiction and the recognition and enforcement of judgments in civil and commercial matters (recast) [2012] OJEU L 351, 1–32.

[7] Indeed, under Art. 1(2)(d) of the Regulation Recast, the 'regulation shall not apply to:…arbitration', and the same concept is confirmed also in Recital No 12.

A closer look at the issue, however, may lead to less certain conclusions, and a more cautious approach seems justified in light of the fact that not only has arbitration not been immune from the debate on conflicts of jurisdictions in Europe,[8] but the debate has focused specifically on matters closely related to arbitration and to the possible clashes between its autonomy[9] and the implications of the principle of mutual trust in Europe.[10] From this perspective, it may be appropriate to reconsider the preliminary conclusion about the irrelevance of Brexit for international commercial arbitration. The question to be addressed, in particular, is whether Brexit may *indirectly* affect international commercial arbitration in Europe and the UK by progressively causing a sceptical attitude amongst domestic courts in EU Member States *vis-à-vis* UK-seated arbitration, on the grounds that post-Brexit UK-seated arbitral tribunals may be more likely to consent to the blatant disregard for EU overriding mandatory rules[11], and post-Brexit UK courts may be less inclined to prevent such daring departure from the European legal orthodoxy.

The extent to which the foregoing is likely to happen will depend primarily on the extent (if any) to which UK law will progressively depart from EU law.[12] However, it will also depend on the perception by domestic courts in EU Member States of the risk of disregard of EU mandatory law by UK-seated arbitral tribunals.

In fact, in the context of international commercial arbitration, the issue of the compatibility between (post-Brexit) UK law and EU mandatory law may be raised *ex post*, at the stage of recognition and enforcement (in an EU Member State) of an award rendered by a UK-seated arbitral tribunal. In this context, and to the extent that the UK-seated arbitral tribunal should overlook the application of EU mandatory law, a defence may be raised against recognition and enforcement of the award on the grounds of an alleged public policy violation under Article V(2)(b) of the New York Convention.[13]

However, the issue of the compatibility between (post-Brexit) UK law and EU mandatory law may also be raised *ex ante*, at the stage of assessment of the

---

[8] See, for instance, Paolo Bertoli, *Diritto Europeo dell'Arbitrato Internazionale* (Milan, Giuffré Editore 2015), 49 ff.

[9] On the autonomy of arbitration, see Markus A Petsche, *The Growing Autonomy of International Commercial Arbitration* (European Law Publishers 2005).

[10] For a recent overview of the issue, see Giles Cuniberti, *Rethinking International Commercial Arbitration: Towards Default Arbitration* (Cheltenham-Northampton 2017).

[11] On the role of EU overriding mandatory rules, see the milestone decision of the CJEU in *Ingmar*: Case C-381/98, *Ingmar GB Limited v Eaton Leonard Technologies Inc* [1998] ECJ I-9325, as well as the immense bibliography commenting on this decision. For an overview of the role of mandatory rules in arbitration, see Luca G Radicati di Brozolo, 'Mandatory Rules and International Arbitration' (2012) 23 Am Rev Int'l Arb 49.

[12] For a similar observation, see Richard Kreindler, Paul Gilbert and Ricardo Zimbron, 'Impact of Brexit on UK Competition Litigation and Arbitration' (2016) 33 J Int'l Arb 521 ff.

[13] On the public policy defense under the New York Convention see, recently, Pascal Hollander, 'Report on the Public Policy Exception in the New York Convention' (2016) 10 Disp Res Int'l 35.

validity of the arbitration agreement.[14] Indeed, to the extent that a court in an EU Member State might find that a given substantive matter is addressed by EU overriding mandatory rules, that court might take that circumstance as a factor justifying, or even imposing the taking of action in order to prevent that the matter be adjudicated outside the EU, on the grounds that this could result in the (unacceptable) circumvention of EU overriding mandatory rules.

In fact, the kind of approach that has just been described is present in recent domestic case-law originating from courts of EU Member States. Indeed, in several cases where the matter in dispute involved the application of EU mandatory provisions, courts of some Member States (including, for instance, Italian[15] and Belgian[16] courts) have reached a negative conclusion as to the *'arbitrability'* of the dispute. Courts of other Member States, in similar circumstances, have reached a substantively comparable conclusion by adopting a pre-emptive approach based on a prognosis of disregard of EU law by the arbitral tribunal, thus retaining their jurisdiction, despite the arbitration agreement, in order to assure the effectiveness of EU law. The latter approach has been adopted, for instance, by German courts,[17] but also by English courts with respect to non-EU seated arbitral tribunals.[18]

Of course, the possibility of an *ex-ante* intervention by courts of EU Member States can be criticized *per se* as too rigid in limiting the operation of party autonomy in international commercial arbitration[19] and, in any event, it can be reasoned that such intervention should be coordinated with the arbitrators' duty to render an award capable of being enforced.[20] It seems correct to argue, however, that the future attitude of domestic courts in Member States of the EU *vis-à-vis* UK-seated arbitration may be affected also (and, maybe, primarily) by the perception of the likelihood that the UK-seated arbitral tribunal will disregard EU mandatory rules and, more generally, by the perception of the possibility of an on-going harmonious (ie, legally coordinated) relationship between the EU and the post-Brexit UK.

---

[14] On this matter, *ex multis*, see Karsten Thorn and Walter Grenz, 'The Effect of Overriding Mandatory Rules on the Arbitration Agreement' in Franco Ferrari and Stefan Kröll (eds), *Conflict of Laws in International Arbitration* (Munich, 2011) 187.

[15] Cf, for instance, Corte di cassazione (Supreme Court of Italy), 30 June 1999 (*Air Malta v Scopelliti Travel Sas*, 2000) Riv Dir Int Priv Proc, 741 ff.

[16] See, for instance, Hof van Cassatie (Supreme Court of Belgium), 3 November 2011 (*Air Transat AT Inc v Air Agencies*), Nr C.10.0613.N <http://jura.juridat.just.fgov.be/pdfapp/download_blob?idpdf=N-20111103-3> accessed 10 June 2017.

[17] Cf Oberlandesgericht (Court of Appeals) Munich, 17 May 2006, Praxis des Internationalen Privat- und Verfahrensrechts (2007) 322 ff; for a comment on this decision, see Giesela Rühl, 'Extending Ingmar to Jurisdiction and Arbitration Clauses: The End of Party Autonomy in Contracts with Commercial Agents?' (2007) Europ Rev Priv L 891 ff.

[18] Cf the decision rendered by the High Court in *Accentuate Limited v Asigra Inc* [2009] EWHC 2655 (QB); also in [2009] 2 Lloyd's Rep 599.

[19] For a comprehensive overview of the issue, see Francesca Ragno, 'Inarbitrability: A Ghost Hovering over Europe?' in Franco Ferrari (ed) *Limits to Party Autonomy in International Commercial Arbitration* (Juris 2016) 127 ff.

[20] Cf Günther J Horvath, 'The Duty of the Tribunal to Render an Enforceable Award' (2001) 18 J Int'l Arb 135 ff.

Among the many factors that may have an impact on the future relationship between the EU and the UK in the field of international commercial arbitration, two will be considered here, due to their apparent capacity to play a relevant role in the matters under consideration.

The first factor relates to the extent to which the exit of the UK from the EU will revive the practice of issuing anti-suit injunctions in support of UK-seated arbitration, whereby the parties are enjoined from bringing a claim before a court of a EU Member State.[21]

In this regard, Brexit (and, in particular, its *hard* version) will most likely cause UK courts to realize very soon that they are no longer bound by the case law of the CJEU, including the ruling against anti-suit injunctions rendered in *West Tankers*,[22] where the court found that such measures are incompatible with the Brussels regime (Reg 44/2001 being in force at the time), because, in essence, they were in conflict with the principle of mutual trust.[23]

It is well known that a heated debate followed the *West Tankers* decision, which had a relevant impact on the decision to amend the Brussels I Regulation. The Proposal presented by the Commission in 2010[24] contained a *lis pendens* rule (Art 29) that would have imposed on the courts of Member States not designated in the arbitration agreement to stay the proceedings once the courts or arbitral tribunals of the designated State were seized. The final version of the Recast Regulation,[25] however, did not adopt the proposed amendment, although Recital 12 (meant to clarify the scope of the persistent '*arbitration exception*' under Art 1(2)(d)) triggered a new debate as to whether the ban against anti-suit injunctions remains in place.[26]

At present, the most convincing and prevailing view is that proceedings which do not come within the scope of the Recast Regulation, may none-

---

[21] On this matter, see Kate Davies and Valeriya Kirsey, 'Anti-Suit Injunctions in Support of London Seated Aribitrations Post-Brexit: Are All Things New Just Well-Forgotten Past?' (2016) 33 J Int'l Arb 501.

[22] Case C-185/07, *Allianz S.p.A. and Generali Assicurazioni S.p.A. v West Takers Inc* [2009] ECR I-663.

[23] For a critical view on this decision, see Alexander Layton, 'Anti-arbitration Injunctions and Anti-suit Injunctions: An Anglo-European Perspective' in Franco Ferrari (ed) *Forum Shopping in the International Commercial Arbitration Context* (Sellier European Law Publishers 2013) 131 ff.

[24] European Commission, 'Proposal for a Regulation of the European Parliament and the Council on jurisdiction and the recognition and enforcement of judgments in civil and commercial matters (Recast)' COM (2010) 748 final.

[25] European Parliament and Council Regulation (EU) No 1215/2012 of 12 December 2012 on jurisdiction and the recognition and enforcement of judgments in civil and commercial matters (recast) OJEU, L 351, 20.12.2012, 1–32.

[26] The issue was recently brought once again to the attention of the CJEU in case C-536/13 (*Gazprom*). On 4 December 2014, the Advocate General Wathelet issued and Opinion holding that under the Recast Regulation, anti-suit injunctions should be regarded as compatible with the legal regime of the EU. The Court, however, didn't uphold this position in its final decision: case C-536/13 *Gazprom OAO v Lietuvos Respublika* [2015] ECLI:EU:C:2015:316.

theless have consequences that undermine the effectiveness of the Brussels regime with regard to the attainment of two distinct objectives:[27] the free movement of decisions and the unification of the rules of conflict of jurisdictions, which requires that courts of all Member States be left free to assess their own jurisdiction under the Regulation. Accordingly, anti-suit injunctions are (still) to be seen as incompatible with the Recast Regulation in that they prevent Member States' courts from applying the rules on the allocation of jurisdiction set forth in the Recast Regulation, thus openly contradicting the principle of mutual trust.[28] A move back to the use of anti-suit injunction by UK courts, in support of UK-based arbitral tribunals, would most likely trigger a countervailing reaction by courts based in EU Member States, which might consider this a sign of the abandonment (not only of the EU, but also) of any willingness to establish a new form of legal cooperation.

Still, the possible move back by UK courts to a more liberal use of anti-suit injunctions in support of arbitration proceedings where a party domiciled in the EU is involved is not the only factor that may lead to an indirect negative impact of Brexit on the role of London as a centre for international commercial arbitration.

A distinct factor should be considered at this point, due to its potential ability to impact on the perception by national courts based in EU Member States of the risk that UK-based arbitral tribunals would overlook EU mandatory rules. This factor relates to the language used by the Arbitration Rules of the London Court of International Arbitration ('LCIA') compared to those of other competing arbitral institutions such as, for instance, the International Chamber of Commerce ('ICC') International Court of Arbitration. The comparison, in fact, may support the argument favouring a pre-emptive intervention by courts based in EU Member States, on the grounds that the LCIA Rules are less stringent in imposing on the arbitrators a duty to render an enforceable award. Indeed, the LCIA's Rules do not require the arbitrators to look into the compatibility of the award with the laws of countries other than that of the arbitral seat. This conclusion is based on the language of Art 32.2 of the LCIA's Rules, which provides that the arbitral tribunal 'shall make every reasonable effort to ensure that any award is legally recognised and enforceable *at the arbitral seat*',[29] thus limiting the scope of the consideration required from arbitrators to the laws of the country of the seat of arbitration.

The corresponding provision contained in Art. 41 of the ICC Rules, by contrast, does not contain any limitation of the scope of the consideration required from the arbitrators to (only) the enforceability of the award at the

---

[27] For this observation, see Pietro Ortolani, 'Anti-suit Injunctions in Support of Arbitration Under the Recast Brussels I Regulation' (2015) Working Paper 6, Max Planck Institute Luxembourg of International, European and Regulatory Procedural Law 5, 13.

[28] This conclusion is supported by Art 45(3) of the Recast Regulation, which sets forth the 'absolute presumption' according to which 'the test of public policy…may not be applied to the rules relating to jurisdiction'.

[29] Emphasis added.

'*arbitral seat*'.[30] In fact, Article 41 of the ICC Rules requires that the arbitral tribunal 'shall make every effort to make sure that the award is enforceable at law', thus requiring that the arbitrators take into account not only the law of the seat of arbitration, but also that of other jurisdictions, including, in particular, those which are in any way connected to the transaction, or to the parties, and those where the recognition and enforcement of the award is likely to be sought.

In other words, after Brexit, the LCIA Rules' reference to the 'arbitral seat' (typically based in the UK) may be perceived as failing to assure the application by the arbitral tribunal of EU overriding mandatory rules and may therefore offer to domestic courts based in EU Member States an argument in favour of retaining jurisdiction notwithstanding an arbitration clause choosing a UK-seated arbitration based on the LCIA Rules.

The resulting uncertainty would clearly have a negative impact on London as a centre for international commercial arbitration, but it would also have a negative impact on international commercial arbitration at large.

Marco Torsello is Associate Professor of Comparative Private Law at the University of Verona (Italy).

---

[30] Similarly, just to provide one additional example, Art 41(2) of the Arbitration Rules of the Singapore International Arbitration Center (the 'SIAC Rules') provides that the arbitral tribunal 'shall make every reasonable effort to ensure...the enforceability of any Award'.

The Effect of Brexit on the UK's Trade with Non-EU Member States Under the EU's Mixed Free Trade Agreements

Robert G. Volterra

1. Introduction

Brexit will have a direct effect on the United Kingdom's ('UK') ability to participate in the European Union's ('EU') external trade arrangements with third countries.[1] This not only includes free trade agreements ('FTAs') signed by the EU within its sphere of exclusive competence but also 'mixed' FTAs signed both by the EU and its Member States in matters of shared competence and other preferential arrangements with third countries (such as the Generalised Schemes of Preferences).[2] According to the House of Commons, the UK has signed and ratified 63 trade agreements with third countries, which account for as much as 20 per cent of the UK's export markets for goods.[3]

2. The status of the parties to mixed EU FTAs under public international law

One of the most controversial questions that has arisen in the wake of Brexit is whether the UK will be able to maintain its participation in the mixed EU FTAs with third countries after it leaves the EU.[4] Commentators who have provided answers to this question diverge considerably in their views.

According to one view, once the UK withdraws from the EU, mixed EU FTAs will automatically terminate with respect to the UK. This is because mixed EU FTAs are essentially 'bilateral' in nature, and the UK will no longer

---

[1] The EU Committee of the House of Lords recently concluded that 'the UK is unlikely to be able to retain access to the EU's FTAs with third countries following Brexit, whether they are mixed agreements or not' (see House of Lords European Union Committee, 'Brexit: the Options for Trade' (5th Report of 2016-17, 2016) Paper 72, para 168 <http://www.publications.parliament.uk/pa/ld201617/ldselect/ldeucom/72/72.pdf> accessed 30 May 2017).

[2] According to the European Commission, the EU already has in place free trade agreements and unilateral trade arrangements with more than 50 trading partners, of both mixed and exclusive competence (see European Commission, 'The EU's Bilateral Trade and Investment Agreements – Where are We?' (3 December 2013) 6 <http://trade.ec.europa.eu/doclib/docs/2012/november/tradoc_150129.pdf> accessed 30 May 2017.

[3] House of Commons Library, 'Legislating for Brexit' (2017) Briefing Paper no 7850, 1–2 <http://researchbriefings.files.parliament.uk/documents/CBP-7792/CBP-7792.pdf> accessed 30 May 2017.

[4] House of Commons Library, 'Brexit: Trade Aspects' (2017) Briefing Paper No. 7694, 30 <http://researchbriefings.parliament.uk/ResearchBriefing/Summary/CBP-7694> accessed 30 May 2017.

qualify as a formal 'party' to these FTAs, particularly under EU law.[5] Others argue that even if the UK remains a 'party' to mixed EU FTAs, these will no longer 'apply' to the UK *ratione personae* and *ratione loci* because mixed EU FTAs restrict the scope of their application to EU Member States, despite the Member States being listed as individual parties to the treaties, or restrict the scope of their application to the territory where the EU treaties apply by virtue of an explicit territorial clause.[6]

Such views appear to contemplate the EU legal regime as a normative framework that supersedes public international law. However, when considering the question of the effect of Brexit on mixed EU FTAs, as a preliminary observation, it must always be recalled that they are international agreements concluded in writing between States. As such, they are treaties governed by the provisions of the Vienna Convention on the Law of Treaties ('VCLT'),[7] or their customary international law equivalent norms.[8] They must be analysed with the understanding that, insofar as they relate to current or future parties, public international law governs their interpretation and application. Accordingly, the determination of who is a 'party' to mixed EU FTAs must be done on the basis of public international law and not EU law.

As such, the UK will continue to qualify as a formal 'party' to most mixed EU FTAs after Brexit. According to Articles 2(1)(f)-(g) and 24 of the VCLT, a State constitutes to be a 'party' to an international treaty so long as it has consented to be bound by the provisions of that treaty,[9] which continues to be in force with respect to it and which has not been terminated in conformity with its

---

[5] Panos Koutrakos, 'Negotiating International Trade Treaties After Brexit' (2016) 41 EL Rev 4, 475–476.

[6] Trade and Investment Law Clinic, 'The Future of the United Kingdom in Europe – Exit Scenarios and Their Implications on Trade Relations' (2014) Papers 2013, 48 <http://graduateinstitute.ch/files/live/sites/iheid/files/sites/ctei/shared/CTEI/Law%20Clinic/Memoranda%202013/Group%20A_The%20Future%20of%20the%20United%20Kingdom%20in%20Europe.pdf> accessed 30 May 2017.

[7] Vienna Convention on the Law of Treaties (adopted 23 May 1969, entered into force 27 January 1980) 1155 UNTS 331 ('VCLT').

[8] Article 3(1)(c) of the VCLT confirms that international agreements concluded between States and other subjects of international law classify as 'treaties', which fall beyond the scope of the VCLT, but may nonetheless be regulated by the provisions of the VCLT with respect to the relations of the contracting States as between themselves. In any event, the VCLT applies directly to most mixed EU FTAs, by virtue of a standard provision whereby they shall be interpreted according to the 'customary rules of interpretation of public international law, including those set out in the [VCLT]'; see, for example, Article 123 of the Economic Partnership Agreement Between the East African Community Partner States, of the one part, and the European Union and its Member States of the other part ('EAC-EU Agreement'); Article 15.18 of the Dispute Settlement Chapter of the Free Trade Agreement between the European Union and the Republic of Singapore ('EU-Singapore FTA'); Article 21 of the Dispute Settlement Chapter of the FREE Trade Agreement between the European Union and the Socialist Republic of Vietnam ('EU-Vietnam FTA'). For the general proposition that mixed EU FTAs must be interpreted in accordance with customary international law, see Case C-386/08 *Firma Brita GmbH v Hauptzollamt Hamburg-Hafen* [2010] ECR 1289, paras 40–45.

[9] Anthony Aust, 'Article 24 Vienna Convention' in Olivier Corten & Pierre Klein (eds) *The Vienna Convention on the Law of Treaties* (OUP 2011) vol I, part II, 629 ('[w]hen a

own terms or the VCLT rules on the termination of treaties.[10] Whilst most mixed EU FTAs contain specific provisions for the termination of their operation, they do not provide for a special termination clause in case of withdrawal of a Member State from the EU. Accordingly, since the UK has signed and ratified these FTAs together with the EU and has not (yet) formally terminated them, it has consented to be bound by the provisions of these FTAs. Those provisions will continue to be in force with respect to it, as the UK will continue to be a 'party' to them under public international law, unless there is an explicit clause in the FTA to the contrary effect.

Hence, the UK's withdrawal from the EU will not, as such, affect its capacity as a formal 'party' to mixed EU FTAs. However, it is true that, from the perspective of EU law, once mixed agreements are concluded by the EU and are duly ratified by the Member States, they become an integral part of the legal system of the Union[11] and come within the scope of EU competence.[12] Thus, the Member States owe an obligation to each other to perform the agreement not simply as a matter of international law but, most importantly, as a matter of EU law (which prevails,[13] pursuant to Article 216(2) of the Treaty on the Functioning of the EU ('TFEU')).[14]

Yet, the relationship between the EU and the Member States under EU law is just a domestic concern from the perspective of third States, which perform the obligations under international mixed agreements on the basis of public international law. Accordingly, if a Member State notifies the EU of its intention to withdraw from the Union, the special relationship under EU law ceases to apply after the period of two years that follows the notification of its intention to withdraw, in conformity with Article 50(3) of the Treaty on the European Union ('TEU') and the default public international law rules apply.

Even if the EU and the UK manage to reach an agreement on the basis of Article 50 of the TEU, this will also not produce any effect *vis-à-vis* third party contracting States. This is because States cannot be bound by the provisions of an agreement between other States without their consent,

---

treaty is in force for a State, including when the treaty enters into force on signature, one should always describe the State as a "party"').

[10] Article 42 of the VCLT introduces a presumption of maintenance of the treaty in force: every treaty concluded and brought into force in accordance with the provisions of Part I of the VCLT shall be considered as being in force and in operation with regard to any State that has signed and ratified it, and it is incumbent upon the party invoking the invalidity, termination, or suspension of the treaty to demonstrate that the ground on which its claim is based, is recognised, and indeed exists in the case at hand. See Marcelo G Kohen & Sarah Heathcote, 'Article 42 1969 Vienna Convention' in Olivier Corten & Pierre Klein (eds) *The Vienna Convention on the Law of Treaties* (OUP 2011) vol II, part V, 1017, and fn 7, with further references.

[11] Case 181/73 *R. & V. Haegeman v Belgian State* [1974] ECR 449, para 5.

[12] Case C-13/00 *Commission v Ireland* [2002] ECR 2943, paras 14–15; Case C-12/86 *Demirel v Stadt Schwäbisch Gmünd* [1987] ECR 3719, para 9.

[13] Case 104/81 *Hauptzollamt Mainz v C.A. Kupferberg & Cie KG a.A.* [1982] ECR 3641, para 13.

[14] Case C-467/98 *Commission v Kingdom Denmark* [2002] ECR I-9519, para 82; Case C-476/98 *Commission v Federal Republic of Germany* [2002] ECR I–9855, para 108.

pursuant to the customary *pacta tertiis* rule, which is reflected in Article 34 of the VCLT[15] and is also binding upon the EU.[16]

3. The scope of application of mixed EU FTAs after Brexit

This does not mean that mixed EU FTAs will 'apply' to the UK automatically either. Whilst the 'entry into force' and the 'application' of a treaty typically coincide, this does not necessarily have to be the case.[17] While a treaty might be in force between two or more States, it might not be applicable with respect to a specific party (*ratione personae*), a specific territory (*ratione loci*), or a set of events situated in time (*ratione temporis*). So the question must be asked again: will mixed FTAs continue to apply to the UK post-Brexit?

There is no 'one-size-fits-it-all' solution to this problem. Each mixed EU FTA must be considered on a case-by-case basis. Each is a separate agreement that needs to be interpreted in accordance with its own wording, taking into account its specific context, its object and purpose, as well as any special meaning that the parties might have intended, pursuant to Article 31 of the VCLT.

It must be emphasized that mixed EU FTAs define their scope *ratione personae* using different wordings. For example, some FTAs enumerate each Member State separately from the EU (of the one part) and the third country (of the other part), hereinafter referred to individually as 'party' and collectively as 'parties'.[18] Other FTAs define the EU and its Member States together as 'the EU, of the one part'.[19] Interestingly, Article 1.1 of the Comprehensive Economic and Trade Agreement ('CETA') defines the parties as 'the European Union *or* its Member States or the European Union *and* its Member States, *within their respective areas of competence* as derived from the [EU Treaties] (hereinafter referred to as the 'EU Party')'.[20]

Different wordings might have different implications for the scope of an FTA's *ratione personae*. For example, where mixed agreements are framed as

---

[15] *Certain German Interests in Polish Upper Silesia (Germany v Poland)*, 1926 PCIJ Series A no 7, May 25, 28-9 ('[a] treaty only creates law as between the States which are parties to it; in case of doubt, no rights can be deduced from it in favour of third States').

[16] The Court of Justice of the EU ('CJEU') has ruled that customary norms of international law are binding on the EU as a whole in Case C-366/10, *Air Transport Association of America v Commission* [2011] ECR I-13755, para 101. The CJEU has applied the customary *pacta tertiis* principle to mixed competence agreements in Case C-386/08 *Firma Brita GmbH v Hauptzollamt Hamburg-Hafen* [2010] ECR 1289, paras 40–45.

[17] Anneliese Quast Mertsch, *Provisionally Applied Treaties: Their Binding Force and Legal Nature* (Martinus Nijhoff, 2012), 123–126.

[18] See, for example, the Preamble of the Economic Partnership Agreement between the West African States, the Economic Community of West African States ('ECOWAS') and the West African Economic and Monetary Union ('UEMOA'), of the one part, and the European Union and its Member States, of the other part.

[19] See, for example, the Preamble of the East African Community ('EAC')-EU Agreement.

[20] Preamble and Article 1.1 of the Comprehensive Economic and Trade Agreement ('CETA') between Canada, of the one part, and the European Union and its Member States, of the other part (emphasis added).

bilateral agreements between 'the EU party' and third States, it could be argued that the intention of the parties was to grant benefits to the EU 'as a whole' only, rather than to the EU as a whole and also individual Member States. In these cases, it could be argued that the context and wording of the FTA portrays an agreement of an 'essentially bilateral nature'.[21] In such cases, even though the UK will formally remain a party to these agreements, the rights which it has enjoyed under their provisions, as well as the obligations it has assumed, may not continue to apply automatically after Brexit.[22] In other words, the provisions of such FTAs might not continue to apply automatically to the UK *ratione personae* post-Brexit.

On the other hand, in different contexts, it might be argued that the Member States have expressed their consent to be bound by these agreements in their 'full rights' as sovereigns,[23] to the extent of some or all of the provisions of the agreement. Thus, the Court of Justice of the EU has held that the division of competences internally within the EU is only a 'domestic question' in which third party States have no need to intervene, 'particularly as it may change in the course of time'.[24]

As noted above, certain FTAs contain a 'territorial clause', which limits their applicability to the territories in which the EU treaties are applied.[25] Such clauses might well result in the non-applicability of mixed EU FTAs to UK territories post-Brexit.[26] It is unclear whether the customary international law rule of 'moving frontiers'[27] might be applied, at least by analogy, to the territorial limitations of the UK's rights and obligations under mixed EU

---

[21] See, for example, Case C-316/91, *Parliament v Council* [1994] ECR I-625, para 3, where the Court ruled that the Fourth Lomé Convention 'established an essentially bilateral ACP-EEC cooperation.'

[22] Panos Koutrakos, 'Editorial – Brexit and international treaty-making' (2016) 1 EL Rev, 1.

[23] The distinction between the EU and the Member States with respect to their status as parties to mixed FTAs at the international level may be paralleled to the distinction between the EU and its Member States as Members to the WTO, which is also an international agreement of mixed competence. The issue was addressed in the case of *EC-Airbus*, where the WTO Panel held that each Member State 'is, *in its own right*, a Member of the WTO, with all the rights and obligations pertaining to such membership,' and '[w]hatever responsibility the European Communities bears for the actions of its member States does not diminish their rights and obligations as WTO Members, but is rather an internal matter concerning the relations between the European Communities and its member States.' See Panel Report, 'European Communities and Certain Member States – Large Civil Aircraft (Airbus)' (1 June 2011) WT/DS316/R, paras 7.174–7.175 (internal references omitted).

[24] Ruling 1/78, 'IAEA Draft Convention on the Physical Protection of Nuclear Materials' [1978] ECR 2151, para 35.

[25] For example, Article 15.15 of the Free Trade Agreement between the European Union and its Member States, of the one part, and the Republic of Korea, of the other part, states that the agreement 'shall apply, on the one hand, to the territories in which the [TEU] and the [TFEU] are applied and under the conditions laid down in those Treaties, and, on the other hand, to the territory of Korea.'

[26] Jed Odermatt, 'Brexit and International Law' (*EJIL:TALK!*, 4 July 2016) <http://www.ejil-talk.org/brexit-and-international-law/> accessed 30 May 2017.

[27] Vienna Convention on Succession of States in Respect of Treaties, 1946 UNTS 3, Article 15. See also Andreas Zimmermann, 'State Succession in Treaties' in *Max Planck Encyclopedia of Public International Law*' (OUP 2006), para 8.

FTAs with third party States.[28] The precise terms of any Brexit agreement might influence the outcome of this issue.

4. Conclusion

The legal fate of mixed EU FTAs will have serious consequences for the progress of the Brexit negotiations. The 'trilateralisation' of mixed EU FTAs could serve as the minimum floor for the negotiating parties and provide a means of dispute settlement in case of controversy, for example. To the extent that the UK remains a 'party' to such FTAs (to any particular extent), it will be able to rely on their provisions to maintain its trade relations with third countries.

Regardless of the resolution of this interesting public international law question, ultimately there are alternatives open to the UK and third party States to structure their affairs prior to Brexit in ways that would enable them to achieve, in legal and practical terms, whatever outcome on which they mutually agree, in relation to the post-Brexit application of the provisions of mixed EU FTAs.[29] There is nothing in the EU legal order or public international law that would prevent understandings in relation to such transitional or 'rollover' agreements from being concluded prior to Brexit. With political will between the UK and any third party States (non-EU, of course), transitional or 'rollover' agreements could provide a quick and simple way for the UK and such States to maintain the *status quo* in terms of trade, pending any post-Brexit renegotiations. This pragmatic approach would provide Brexit-stability in terms of trade for businesses based in and trading with the UK (outside the EU 27).

Robert G. Volterra is Visiting Professor of Law at
University College London and partner at the public law
international law firm Volterra Fietta.[30]

---

[28] For a similar argument in the context of the EU Member States' Schedules of Concessions under the General Agreement on Trade in Services in the Context of the WTO, see Lorand Bartels, 'The UK's status in the WTO after Brexit' (SSNR, 23 September 2016) 12–13 <https://www.peacepalacelibrary.nl/ebooks/files/407396411.pdf> accessed 30 May 2017.

[29] In February 2017, the UK Government reassured that it seeks to achieve continuity in its trade relationships with third countries, 'including those covered by existing EU FTAs', and confirmed that it is exploring ways to ensure maximum continuity and certainty as well as preferential arrangements for developing countries. See Department for Exiting the EU and Department for International Trade, 'Brexit – the Options for Trade: Government Response' (28 February 2017) <https://www.parliament.uk/documents/lords-committees/eu-external-affairs-subcommittee/Future-trade-EU-UK-Government-Response-and-Annex%20A.pdf> accessed 30 May 2017.

[30] The author is grateful for the assistance of his colleague Emmanuel Giakoumakis in preparing this article.

Empty Threats: Why the United Kingdom Has Currently No Chance to Become a Tax or Regulatory Haven

Luca Enriques

Immediately after the European Union ('EU') referendum, a French commentator predicted that, after Brexit, the United Kingdom ('UK') would likely become a regulatory and/or tax haven by lowering corporate taxes and deregulating its economy to attract relocations from the Continent and elsewhere.[1] Even out of the EU, the UK would still have the advantages of proximity to the largest economic free trade area on the planet and perhaps, depending on the outcome of the negotiations, of still being associated with it one way or the other. A few days later, George Osborne, then still fully in charge as Chancellor of Exchequer, appeared to have plans consient with that prediction, as he announced his intention to lower the corporate income tax rate to 15 %, which would be the lowest among large economies.[2]

Following his replacement with Philip Hammond a few days later in Theresa May's cabinet, that plan was apparently abandoned. But some six month later, in her Lancaster House speech, Theresa May explicitly used the tax/regulatory haven option as a counter-threat to those 'voices calling for a punitive deal that punishes Britain and discourages other countries from taking the same path'.[3] In her own words, 'Britain would not – indeed [they] could not – accept such an approach,'[4] famously adding that 'no deal for Britain is better than a bad deal for Britain', and then stating: 'Because we would still be able to trade with Europe. We would be free to strike trade deals across the world. *And we would have the freedom to set the competitive tax rates and embrace the policies that would attract the world's best companies and biggest investors to Britain. And – if we were excluded from accessing the Single Market – we would be free to change the basis of Britain's economic model'.*[5]

---

[1] Anne Michel, 'Londres, futur paradis fiscal de l'Europe?' *Le Monde* (Paris, 25 June 2016) <http://www.lemonde.fr/idees/article/2016/06/25/londres-futur-paradis-fiscal-de-l-europe_4958090_3232.html> accessed 20 June 2017.

[2] George Parker, 'George Osborne puts corporation tax cut at heart of Brexit recovery plan' *Financial Times* (London, 3 July 2016) <https://www.ft.com/content/d5aedda0-412e-11e6-9b66-0712b3873ae1> accessed 20 June 2017.

[3] Speech from Theresa May (Lancaster House, 17 January 2017) <http://www.telegraph.co.uk/news/2017/01/17/theresa-mays-brexit-speech-full> accessed 20 June 2017.

[4] ibid.

[5] ibid (emphasis added). There is no trace of such a threat in the White Paper on Brexit. See Department for Exiting the European Union, 'The United Kingdom's exit from and new partnership with the European Union' (2017) <https://www.gov.uk/government/publications/the-united-kingdoms-exit-from-and-new-partnership-with-the-european-union-white-paper> accessed 20 June 2017.

The Financial Times was quick to dismiss Theresa May's 'Plan B' (turning the UK into a 'Singapore of the west') as an 'empty' threat that would never be executed upon, given its inconsistency with May's far from neo-liberal political philosophy.[6] As I write, the political days of Theresa May as UK Prime Minister appear to be numbered, so one may wonder: would that Plan B become more credible under a new Prime Minister with less of a distaste for pro-business policies, such as, for instance, Boris Johnson?[7] The simple answer is 'no', and not because a Boris Johnson Cabinet would necessarily be unlikely to execute on it, but because, even if it did, Plan B would be unlikely to harm the EU and its Member States.

In the present political environment, the UK is in fact highly unlikely to attract any significant number of foreign businesses.[8] Relocating is costly. If a UK location is no longer cost-effective down the road, for instance because the relevant policies are changed, a second relocation will be needed, adding to the cost of the prior one. Hence, businesses will bear the costs of moving to the UK only if they can be persuaded that the new attractive tax and legal environment is there to stay. The problem is that the UK is not currently in a position to credibly commit to such a stable business-friendly environment.

Jurisdictions attracting foreign business with favourable tax or legal treatment (think of Luxembourg or Delaware) tend to have relatively small economies, where the revenues for the State from the economic activity generated by the favourable tax or regulatory regimes are a significant portion of the total. That makes the State's commitment credible, because the harm to public finances from reneging on the promise to maintain the favourable *status quo* would be huge and, as a consequence, the political system can be expected not to meddle with the existing arrangements.[9]

A large economy like the UK's is thus at a disadvantage from this point of view. Yet, countervailing factors may still allow a large country to attract a disproportionate amount of economic or financial activity within its borders. After all, the City of London has attracted financial activities from all over the world for decades despite the large size of the UK's economy. That is not to say that the UK won the competition in financial services via regulatory or tax dumping. It means, rather, that the UK was eventually able to credibly commit to preserving the quality of its regulatory and tax environment over the long run.

---

[6] George Parker, Jonathan Ford and Alex Barker, 'Is Theresa May's Brexit Plan B an elaborate bluff?' *Financial Times* (London, 19 January 2017) <https://www.ft.com/content/3501446a-de36-11e6-86ac-f253db7791c6> accessed 20 June 2017.

[7] See, eg, Alexander Temerko, 'Boris Johnson is the best hope for the Tories – and for Britain' *The Guardian* (London, 24 March 2016) <https://www.theguardian.com/commentis-free/2016/mar/24/boris-johnson-hope-tories-britain> accessed 20 June 2017 – where Boris Johnson is described as 'staunchly pro-business'.

[8] Depending on the magnitude of the dumping, however, it may succeed in retaining existing UK-based businesses, which is not, of course, what the threat is about.

[9] See, eg, Roberta Romano, 'Law As a Product: Some Pieces of the Incorporation Puzzle' (1985) 1 J Law Econ Organ 231-35.

How did it do it? There are, of course, many explanations. But arguably, in the past decades, the appeal of the City as a financial centre owed much to the high quality, stability, and trustworthiness of UK institutions. A long tradition of parliamentary democracy, the rule of law, independent courts, stable governments, free and inquisitive media, a strong legal profession and, relatively speaking, a predictable, largely moderate electorate that could be expected not to be willing to renounce the advantages of hosting a highly profitable financial centre all played an essential part in the City's success.

The context is now different. First came the diffused, and (arguably) justified, anger against bankers following the financial crisis. While UK policymakers were arguably no harsher than others in reshaping financial regulation, there can be no presumption that a pro-business and/or pro-financial institutions agenda would not be severely punished at the next general election. Then, and relatedly, the EU referendum has given a severe blow to the UK's political institutions' credibility. To an external observer, the very decision to ask such a complicated (and open-ended) question to the electorate via a simple majority vote looks reckless.[10] The quality of the EU Referendum campaign debate and coverage was surprisingly dismal, while the low instincts and fleeting emotions of the enraged majority in favour of Leave[11] entail a degree of unpredictability in British politics that was hitherto unacknowledged.[12] Furthermore, the cluelessness of politicians about what to do after the unexpected outcome, and, more generally, the messy state of post-referendum national politics,[13] added a final touch of amateurism to an already grim picture. But when things appeared to be back on track under the proclaimed strong and stable leadership of Theresa May, there came, first, the puzzling refusal to obtain the Parliament's approval before triggering Article 50, which added a touch of surrealism to the framework of a constitutional order in which the only certainty is its Parliament's sovereignty, and required the pronouncement of the UK Supreme Court.[14] And then, just after Parliament had authorized Brexit in 130 words, a snap election called to strengthen the UK Government's position in the Brexit negotiations produced a hung Parliament and the surge in popularity of an old-style Marxist.

---

[10] See, eg, Kenneth Rogoff, 'Britain's democratic failure' *Project Syndicate* (Prague, 24 June 2016) <https://www.project-syndicate.org/commentary/brexit-democratic-failure-for-uk-by-kenneth-rogoff-2016-06> accessed 20 June 2017.

[11] See Leaders, 'The Politics of Anger' *The Economist* (London, 2 July 2016) <http://www.economist.com/news/leaders/21701478-triumph-brexit-campaign-warning-liberal-international-order-politics?frsc=dg%7Cc> accessed 20 June 2017.

[12] It is of no relief that voters are not acting more rationally elsewhere. Even leaving aside the recent important exceptions of core EU countries such as France and the Netherlands, the point here is whether one could trust voters to act more rationally in the UK than elsewhere.

[13] George Parker and Alex Barker, 'Intrigue and betrayal stalk UK's corridors of power' *Financial Times* (London, 1 July 2016) <https://www.ft.com/content/1e4bc772-3f71-11e6-9f2c-36b487ebd80a> accessed 20 June 2017.

[14] *R (Miller) v Secretary of State for Exiting the European Union* [2017] UKSC 5.

In short, the post-EU referendum uncertainty relates not only to the future of UK/EU relationships, but also to the stability and trustworthiness of British political institutions. That uncertainty may not be enough to erode the competitive advantages for firms that are already established in the UK (for them, relocating elsewhere will be a certain cost to be compared to the uncertain ones of remaining where they are), but makes any attempt to attract new businesses or to rebrand the UK as a tax or regulatory haven at the border of the EU extremely unlikely to succeed.

To conclude, EU negotiators should be unimpressed if ever their UK counterparts threaten to turn the UK into a tax and/or regulatory haven: even if the UK really went down that road, in the post-EU referendum political environment it would attract very little business.

Luca Enriques is the Allen & Overy Professor
of Corporate Law at the University of Oxford,
Faculty of Law.

Brexit Arithmetics

Kalypso Nicolaidis

Red lines, packages, positions, 'no deal', concessions, hard-line, bluff – the early stages of the Brexit negotiations between the United Kingdom ('UK') government and its European Union ('EU') counterparts did not bode well for what is still to come. Clearly, neither side seemed to find the vocabulary, tactics, and vision to engage in positive-sum or integrative bargaining, the art of creating value at the same time as you share it, the 101 of any good negotiator.[1] As this book goes to press in the Summer of 2017, a year after the referendum, we know a bit more about the two sides' stated positions and purported 'red lines' beyond the Prime Minister's infamous 'Brexit means Brexit'.[2] Yet the end-game is harder to predict than with any standard multi-party, multi-level, multi-issue negotiations, simply because the parties don't seem to agree on what kind of game they are playing in the first place, either between the two sides or internally. All that is clear is that the result will depend less on what the UK wants and more on what the rest of the other 27 EU members ('EU27') will give.

Nevertheless, I try to demonstrate here that the fundamentals are simple enough to be described in three short equations, each of which gives us a clue about an eventual Deal UK ('Duk'). This simplifying gimmick can also be used to ask what an integrative approach to these history-making negotiations may entail.

1. Equation 1: Vm > Duk > Vnfm

This equation states that the general value of Duk cannot be greater than the value of EU membership (Vm), but that it could be greater than existing deals with non-former members ('Vnfm') such as Norway, Switzerland, Turkey or Canada.

On the first side of the equation – Vm > Duk – we find a statement of fact that is obvious on the EU side but not on the British side – in fact, isn't the Brexit bet the exact opposite proposition: ie, that the Duk that will eventually

---

[1] As we have taught at Harvard for the last four decades: see ia, Howard Raiffa, *The art and science of negotiation* (HUP, 1982); David Lax, *The Manager as negotiator* (Simon and Schuster, 1987); Kalypso Nicolaidis, 'Power and Negotiation: When should lambs negotiate with lions?' in Deborah Kolb (ed), *Negotiating Eclectics: Essays in Memory of Jeffrey Z. Rubin* (1999) 102–119.

[2] For a journey on what this may mean, as Brexit Mythology, see Kalypso Nicolaidis, 'Exodus, Reckoning, Sacrifice: Three Meanings of Brexit' (Unbound-Random House, *forthcoming*).

be struck, with all of the margins of freedom for the UK that will thus open up, will be better than the value of membership? There lies the first fundamental paradox of these negotiations. Clearly, this divergence can only work because the two sides make different bets about the future. But then again, this is not a bet about the weather, but about a state of affairs where all sides have agency.

To restate the root of mutual misperceptions: For the EU, this is a truism; it would be absurd for Brussels to offer a deal to a third-country-to-be that is more valuable than the value of membership itself. When this is uttered in a neutral legalistic fashion, 'more valuable' refers to the package of rights and obligations associated with membership vs non-membership. The membership ticket must be worth something! But the message sent is not the message received: the British side hears this EU statement as a desire to 'punish' the UK. But how can they hear this, if they understand the basic need for membership to have value? Well, this UK perception is not totally absurd, if we consider a broader take on Duk that is not just the formal legal-political deal but the outcome of that deal, something rather more amorphous that aggregates the formal deal with its symbolic, economic, and political consequences. EU negotiators would be hard-pressed to deny that the value of Duk is also about precedent and *pour decourager les autres* – 'we cannot make Brexit a success' is at least for some an implicit mantra, which makes it hard to separate legal from material considerations.

And who could blame them: like any club managing 'commons', the EU must protect itself against free-riding. For most clubs, benefits can spill over to outsiders, and it is unfair for these outsiders to benefit without contributing at all. The UK cannot, therefore, get a better deal now than David Cameron was offered in February 2016 as an enticement for the British public to want to stay in. Concessions on free movement will need to cost enough in other areas to highlight the value of membership. The problem with the Brits as seen from Paris is that they are, well, too French: *ils veulent le beurre, l'argent du beurre et baiser la fermiere* (loosely translatable as 'wanting to have their cake, eat it, and kiss the baker's wife too'). The Brexiteers must hear this straightforward reasoning. But the EU27 also need to ask themselves whether such a mindset does not simply show the EU as insecure and *petite*. Should people want to stay in the EU for fear of bad consequences if they leave, or would the EU not simply be more attractive if it was seen as magnanimous and grand in its dealing with its first departing member?!

Which brings us to the other side of the equation – VDuk > Vnfm – which may be the key to positive-sum Brexit negotiations. The suggestion that Duk ought to be better than the deals granted to countries that have never been EU members, encapsulates the assumption that we need to build a unique special partnership. Lets ponder this proposition for a moment: a new species of State is conjured up with Brexit, namely the 'former EU Member State'. Would it not debase the status of such membership to treat the UK worse than those who have never been equals around the EU table, who do not know 'our' (the EU's) grand strategies and all 'our' (the EU's) dirty little secrets, whose diplomats and civil servants have never contributed sweat and tears to promoting the EU agenda in the rest of the world for the last four decades, and (some of) whose politicians across the political spectrum have not courageously tried to promote the EU case against a relentless tabloid press? Would it not debase the status of EU citizenship if it could be lost so easily, EU citizen one morning, non-EU citizen the next! The European Court of Justice ('ECJ') has already ruled that citizenship of an EU Member State ought not to be lost easily. Things are of course different for the future citizens of a 'former Member State' – but this no-man's land with no precedent needing to be explored.[3]

Moreover, we all know that 'Great' Britain is not any old state and must be allowed to save face. This last consideration is never made explicit on the continent but is nevertheless part of Europe's historical memory.

Add to these substantive points the simple facts that the UK will be negotiating while still a member and that the marginal cost for the EU of undoing complex internal and external bargains that have included the UK in the last 42 years may be higher than the marginal benefit of 'demonstrating' that leaving is costly. This all increases the plausibility of models like 'European Economic Area plus', or something else, like a different kind of a membership in a club of clubs.[4]

In all this, atmospherics matter as much as pragmatics. A (British) divorce was always going to be less friendly than a (Swiss) flirt. So it is also conceivable that the UK's demands might appear so outlandish, and its tone so arrogant, that no one will care anymore about recognising its special status as a former Member State or European great power. Especially if it uses as a bargaining chip the threat of a race to the bottom on such policies as corporate taxation, the continent's willingness to cut it slack will swiftly diminish. This would be freeriding in its purest form and represent an admission that the UK has jettisoned any respect for the basic premises of the EU. In this case, why should Duk be better than deals granted to, say, EEA partners who respect the EU's rule of the game with very little input of their own? The equation could become: Vm > Vnfm> Duk.

Would Duk remain better than 'no deal', even under these circumstances? Arguably, yes, given the unattractiveness of the UK's BATNA ('best alternative to a negotiated agreement') – not only in a World Trade Organisation ('WTO') world where global rules are a moving target, but in being the only

---

[3] See Patricia Mindus, 'A Sudden Loss of Rights' in *European Citizenship after Brexit* (Springer International Publishing, 2017) 29–43; Catherine Barnard, 'Theresa May claimed her offer to EU citizens would be 'generous.' It isn't' *The Guardian* (London, 27 June 2017) <https://www.theguardian.com/commentisfree/2017/jun/27/theresa-may-offer-generous-eu-citizens-tories-rights-uk> accessed 2 July 2017.

[4] Giandomenico Majone, *Rethinking the union of Europe post-crisis: has integration gone too far?* (CUP 2014).

EU neighbour without privileged ties. This prospect would be bad for the EU too, of course. Unfortunately, how the 'no deal' alternative plays out in these negotiations will depend on whether parties care about relative or absolute gains – if the UK hurts more, the EU might throw its hands up and decree, *inshallah*!

2. Equation 2: Duk = FI – CP

The second equation about the specifics of the deal is even more straightforward. Duk will likely allow the UK to opt in to aspects of the EU membership which are earmarked for 'flexible integration' ('FI'), but the EU 27 will resist British attempts to cherry-pick ('CP') its favourite aspects of membership without any wider rationale. For instance, it might be ok to selectively participate in EU research networks or defence procurement, but not ok to opt out from regional funds which help Europe's poorest regions, or from the bits of product standards linked to the single market that the UK does not like.

In the next few years, flexible integration or differentiation will be key for the EU, even more than it has been until now (EMU, Schengen). If the EU is to survive, its policy and institutions must reflect what it has become: a continent-wide ensemble of heterogeneous states and economies which show little sign of convergence. The rationale matters to the UK deal: if the same EU laws and institutions affect different states differently, we need flexible integration – opt-ins rather than opt-outs. As with affirmative action, which is meant to compensate a disproportionate disadvantage from undifferentiated laws for a minority in society, the UK could claim that its special circumstances warrant an extensive exploration of the potential for differentiated integration and that its case could be an icebreaker in this regard. Perhaps non-euro (still) Member States might want to join it in this new kind of quasi-membership.

But there is a fine line between such flexible integration and what the EU diehards ominously refer to as cherry picking (choosing your favourite policy solely on grounds of what works for you). It is around defining this fine line that much of the negotiations will hinge – an art the British side has yet to master. You want EU partners on board with some sort of *a la carte* exit? Figure out when does (good) differentiation stop and (bad) exceptions start. Avoid idiosyncratic, *ad-hoc* demands and find arguments based on generalizable principles. Part of the problem with the early phase of negotiations controlled by the former Home office supremo is that Theresa May's only experience of the EU pertained to a field, Justice and Home Affairs ('JHA'), that had been among the most flexible in the EU legal landscape, allowing the UK to carve micro-opt-ins where it had previously claimed macro-opt-outs. No wonder that the Junkers of this world thought she was on a 'different galaxy' – she was in the JHA universe! Maybe she saw the EU at its best – allowing for the utter diversity of its Member States.

When (good) differentiation stops and (bad) exceptions start will be an-swered differently across areas of negotiations. The answer depends in part on whether one believes, as I do, in a 'demoicratic' EU which flexibly adapts to the complex realities of its Member States.[5] There will be a need to revisit what I call 'the construction of indivisibility' between the four freedoms which for most of the EU's history were connected substantively, and even linked strategically, but do not by their economic nature need to come in an indivisible bundle. There will be discussions about the difference between 'equivalence', which can be granted to the UK, and mutual recognition, which is a more exclusive privilege – but what if the real difference is that the latter can be revoked unilaterally? Why not stay with recognition if the mix of trust and monitoring which it requires can be obtained with a UK whose starting point is to have been recognized already?[6] There will be discussions on the EU budget about the difference between solid commit-ments and contingent liabilities, but, at the end of the day, who can doubt that principles will be twisted to accommodate the need for side-payments? And there will be critical discussions about how sticky, in principle, should EU citizenship rights be – an area where principles matter, when sixty per cent of British citizens would be willing to pay to retain their EU citizenship.[7]

Some will argue that differentiated integration is backdoor membership, while others will ask: what is wrong with that? The real problem will be who decides where the frontier lies between FI and CP. As the French see it, the Brits continue to yearn for bits of the menu *gourmand* and bits of the menu *touristique*. Fear not! You can choose among menus, but we choose what the menus are. As the Germans see it, however, better to have the Brits stay and eat at our restaurant, even if we need to cater the offerings. How the rest of Europe will side on this one might be critical.

3. Equation 3: Duk = Min (U+B) + Max (M)

This equation turns to the institutional approach adopted in the negotiations and states that Duk must maximize multilateralism ('M') and minimize unilateral ('U'), or bilateral ('B') approaches. With an EU based on the rule of law, there is precious little room for either of the latter. And where there may be some room, it should be used judiciously.

The pro-Leave camp in the UK sees unilateralism as the first step to 'independence': the absorption of British law by India when becoming independent from its British masters provides the best model for the so called 'Great Repeal Act' which will integrate all EU laws with an option to

---

[5] Richard Bellamy and Sandra Kröger, 'A demoicratic justification of differentiated integration in a heterogenous EU' (2017) 39 J Eur Integrat.

[6] For a discussion see ia, Kalypso Nicolaidis, 'Mutual Recognition in the Shadow of Brexit' (*forthcoming*) 70 *Current Legal Problems*.

[7] LSE research initiative for the study of electoral psychology, ECREP, in conjunction with polling firm Opinium, 4 July 2017.

revise; the Corn Laws which enforced the UK's unilateral free trade stance between 1815 and 1846 demonstrate the wisdom of unilateral trade disarmament and show the way to a new UK, free to open its markets to imports from around the world unshackled from the EU's common tariffs, etc.

But aside from the irony of the Indian story, UK politicians have had to learn, not least from their own negotiators, who know better, that unilateral openness means little in a world where trade is not mainly about tariffs, but is underpinned by the mutual recognition of standards which are constantly and collectively updated, interpreted, and litigated. Even if EU laws were copied-and-pasted into British law via the 'Great Repeal Bill' (or better, the 'Great Repeat Act'), that would mean little without the cooperation mechanisms which make them operative as access tickets to the EU's single market. And as far as unilateral threats of competitive regulation and devaluation, they either lack credibility when they amount to self-harm (tax intake or regulatory protection) or lack in effectiveness when they would simply invite retaliation from a much more powerful EU.

In truth, unilateralism can only work when it serves as signalling, as a show of goodwill – something the UK could have done sooner with the status of EU citizens in Britain: in this case, simply extending their right to stay without asking for anything in exchange would have bought much more goodwill on the treatment of retired British citizens in the EU than using them as bargaining chips.

Similarly, bilateralism seems to have been an early cognitive frame, starting with a British foreign minister threatening the Italians with an import ban on Prosecco. That is to misunderstand the logic of trade negotiations in the EU, which have been structured to allow no less cherry-picking between countries than between issues. Sure, there is lobbying within and by each Member State – but their individual stance eventually has to come together in a single position. Indeed, by delegating negotiation authority to Michel Barnier, the EU has sought to pre-empt what it sees as the 'divide-and-rule' *modus operandi* of the UK. But too much unity on the part of the EU would be a mistake. There is nothing wrong with the fact that the UK does have variable geometry relationships with many of the Member States, from Spain to where it exports its sunshine-friendly oldies, to Poland from whom it imports those who care for the oldies who stayed put. These ties cannot be leveraged against the EU, but must be harnessed to build a better, kinder Brexit.

More generally, the EU's commitment to regional multilateralism is, of course, what defines it as a community predicated on replacing specific reciprocity with diffuse reciprocity based on collective rules (say agreeing on EU competition policy where the EU regulates anti-competitive behaviour on everyone's behalf, instead of allowing everyone to apply to anti-dumping).[8] At the end of the day, the EU's economic constitution is about transforming

---

[8] William Phelan, *In place of inter-state retaliation: The European Union's rejection of WTO-style trade sanctions and trade remedies* (OUP 2015).

defensive trade weapons into both common rules and compensations, including subsidies to poorer regions that might benefit less than others from the single market. The more Britain is perceived as adopting what Europeans see as a transactional approach and ignoring the EU's rules of the game, the less goodwill will remain in European capitals when the time comes to strike Duk.

Multilateralism may be antithetic to the 'currency of control' worshiped by Brexiteers, but they have little choice. And if they have, four decades of membership in this Union have created a deep degree of co-ownership of the multilateral rules that the UK itself greatly contributed in shaping. This historical responsibility, in turn, ought to constrain its manner of leaving, to the extent that Brexit will affect the countries' respective ability to manage collective action problems on both sides.[9] Why behave as if the country has already unlearned the lessons of four decades of membership? Conversely, should the EU insist that the new structures that manage the relationship post-Brexit be the same or clones of its own, asking for the Brexit agreement to 'respect the role of the Court of Justice of the European Union' as if somehow you cannot leave the ECJ, like Hotel California?

The Brexit deal needs to invent a new kind of multi-normative multilateralism befitting the new state of affairs. Whether the Brexit talks follow the logic of trade negotiations, with Barnier and the Commission, the logic of Council negotiations, with Merkel and Macron, or the logic of climate negotiations, with broader bottom-up consultations, such negotiations will be multilateral and perhaps borrow from all these shared experiences.

In the end, it may be that the specific modalities associated with membership for a future 'out-almost-in' UK do not differ widely from the specific modalities associated with its prior status of being 'in-almost-out'. Some argue that Brexit will not make a damn bit of difference.[10] I have argued that the parameters of the negotiations are such that, on the contrary, there is plenty of margin for interpretation and empathy in this vastly consequential games, and that if the parties are to avoid leaving too much value on the table, they will need to compare and contrast more systematically their respective takes on the basics of Brexit arithmetics.[11]

Kalypso Nicolaidis is Professor of International Relations and Director of the Center for International Studies at the University of Oxford.

---

[9] Chris Lord 'The Legitimacy of Exits in the European Union' (2017) 39 J Eur Integrat.

[10] Simon Jenkins, 'Soft Brexit is the only sane option' *The Guardian* (London, 30 June 2017).

[11] An earlier version of this article was published in January 2017 by the European Council for Foreign Relations (Kalypso Nicolaidis, 'Brexit arithmetics: a logical approach to predicting a Brexit deal' in *EU Referendum and Brexit: Analysis* (European Council on Foreign Relations, 2017) <http://www.ecfr.eu/article/commentary_a_logical_approach_to_predicting_a_brexit_deal_7217> accessed 2 July 2017).

Triggering Article 50 – Strategic Approaches to Brexit Negotiations

Owen Darbishire

The triggering of Article 50 by Theresa May on 29 March 2017 represented not the start of the Brexit negotiation process, but the end of the first, preparatory phase. During the subsequent stages of active negotiations, there remain many deep political and technical challenges. The complexity of the negotiations is compounded by their potential to destroy significant value. They are not simply 'value creating' negotiations. In both trade and political terms, a core challenge is to minimise the losses that occur. There exist many possible outcomes, from the substantive risks of no agreement to the even greater likelihood that any outcome will be suboptimal from the perspective of both principal parties.[1]

The challenges in devising suitable negotiation strategies include their multi-level, multi-lateral nature, amplified by there being multiple separate negotiations with distinct process rules, including the Article 50 'divorce' negotiations and the trade negotiations. Beyond these lie the substantial linkage effects across a broad array of dimensions from reputations and relationships, to symbolism and precedents, and on to future European Union ('EU') budget negotiations and even Scottish and Irish politiscal settlements.

The preparatory phase of the negotiations did nothing to increase the grounds for optimism. Understanding why can give insights into dimensions that need particular care and attention over the 18 months from 19 June 2017 when active negotiations are scheduled.

While all negotiations have significant substantive and analytical dimensions, the nature of communication and emotions remain highly pertinent, no more so where the negotiations have considerable political and even existential implications. The framing of the first phase of the Brexit negotiations was wanting in these respects.[2] Indeed, the United Kingdom ('UK') approach was narrow and at times myopic. Initiating a negotiation without preparation, with negligible understanding of the complex dimensions, and with simultaneously unclear and contradictory objectives is inevitably problematic. This set the stage for flaws in the UK's approach.

The internal UK contest to influence the strategic goals and preferences for the negotiations following the referendum result in June 2016 led to much exagger-

---

[1] Howard Raiffa, *The Art and Science of Negotiation: How to Resolve Conflicts and Get the Best Out of Bargaining* (Cambridge: Harvard University Press 1982).

[2] William A Donohue, Randall G Rogan, and Sandra Kaufman, *Framing Matters: Perspectives on Negotiation Research and Practice in Communication* (New York: Peter Lang 2011).

ated and simplistic analysis and rhetoric. This combined with an over-optimism bias and self-serving evaluations,[3] especially in the extent to which the substantive advantages of a trade deal would dominate the EU27 decision-making. Yet the many public pronouncements from key political figures such as Boris Johnson, David Davis and Liam Fox were not confined to domestic consumption as they sought to influence the internal political debate and structure attitudes.[4] Beyond this, statements have communication and emotional consequences within the EU27. This is closely related to the criticality of understanding the perspective of the other party, which has been largely absent from the UK's positioning and yet has substantial impacts on negotiations outcomes.[5] Both dimensions needed (and need) much more careful management.

Considerable attention was focused on the balance of power by both the UK and the EU27. Control over critical resources and process undoubtedly matter. However, the nature of power, which is fundamentally about being able to move an outcome in a desired direction, is more subtle than has been understood.[6] This is particularly so as the situation changes from a two-party negotiation to a multi-party, multi-level one. In this context, power does not relate only to the dynamics between the UK and the EU27. It also relates to the internal, multi-level negotiations. Overall, power becomes the ability to manage the multiple dimensions towards a successful conclusion. It is thus entirely possible for one or both parties to constrain their own freedom of action through the commitments made to internal constituencies. In turn, this can shrink the feasible settlement zone, destroying potential resolutions to difficult conflicts, and increasing the chances of a 'pareto sub-optimal' outcome. The drawing of strong 'red lines' (such as over the role of the European Court of Justice) and commitments to core constituencies as to what will be achieved and accepted can, therefore, leave both principal parties finding that they have too little power. Achieving good outcomes in negotiations is seldom achieved with 'absolutes'. The art of managing internal expectations was insufficient during the preparatory phase, leaving an additional challenge for the active negotiation phases.

In seeking to increase bargaining leverage, the UK declined to take unilateral action with regards EU citizens' rights, seeing them as 'bargaining chips', while indicating the use of security, defence and terrorism capabilities to the same end. The dominant analytical method in negotiations advocates maximising the trade-offs among issues according to relative preferences to optimise outcomes, while following the guidance that 'nothing is agreed until

---

[3] Chia-Jung Tsay and Max H Bazerman, 'A decision-making perspective to negotiation: A review of the past and a look into the future' (2009) 25(4) Negotiation J 467–480.

[4] Richard E Walton and Robert B McKersie, *A Behavioural Theory of Labor Negotiations: An Analysis of a Social Interaction System* (New York: McGraw Hill 1965).

[5] Adam D Galinsky, William W Maddux, Debra Gilin, and Judith B White, 'Why It Pays to Get Inside the Head of Your Opponent: The Differential Effects of Perspective Taking and Empathy in Negotiations' (2008) 9(4) Psychol Sci 378–384.

[6] I William Zartman and Jeffrey Z Rubin (eds), *Power and Negotiation* (Ann Arbor: The University of Michigan Press 2002).

everything is agreed'.[7] While having much merit, such interest-based bargaining is not without its limits. This is so where such an approach undermines stated objectives to build a new partnership, is questioned from a moral rights or legitimacy perspective, and/or is perceived as a hard-bargaining approach which heightens the risk of eliciting reciprocal actions. Together, these greatly increase the risk that behaviourally the negotiations become a 'distributive,' value claiming power play. The Brexit negotiations encompass a vast array of issues and interests from financial services to fisheries and so on, each of which contains many sub-issues and interests. The art is to identify where interest-based bargaining can be legitimately and successfully applied.

The tense relationship between the UK and the EU27 has amplified the tendency to adopt power-based approaches, not least with the EU27 placing a moratorium on informal negotiations prior to the formal triggering of Article 50. Doing so successfully maintained cohesion among the 27, as well as the critical negotiation tactic of control over the process, which thus sustains the power advantages inherent in the design of Article 50.[8] Ramping up power-based negotiations tactics, including the UK issuing implicit threats of adopting a 'Singapore' economic model, do nothing to lead to a well designed process that maximises the chances of a successful outcome for any party. The questionable credibility of such threats do not, however, prevent them from increasing the complexity of the negotiations as steps are taken to further protect interests which would be of less significance in a relationship based upon partnership.

If the Article 50 and subsequent free trade agreement negotiations are to be successful, they require critical shifts in approach by both the UK and the EU27. The power-based positional approaches that dominated the preparatory phase combined with a narrowly focused understanding of mutual interests. To be successful, negotiators need to manage internal expectations carefully and adopt a clear understanding of the perspective of the other side. Even more critically, they have to consider creative options that will be of mutual benefit, which is fundamental to successful negotiations in politically complex situations. The absence of these preconditions does not mean that there will be no agreement. The challenge, however, is how to reach an agreement of high quality recognising the core political constraints on both sides. The design of the process only increases this challenge.

Owen Darbishire is the Rhodes Trust Associate Professor in Management Studies (Organisational Behaviour and Industrial Relations) at Saïd Business School, University of Oxford.

---

[7] Roger Fisher, William L Ury, and Bruce M Patton, *Getting to Yes: Negotiating an Agreement Without Giving In* (revised 2nd ed, Random House 1991).

[8] David A Lax and James K Sebenius, *3-D Negotiation: Powerful Tools to Change the Game in Your Most Important Deals* (Boston MA: Harvard Business School Press 2006).

Creating Value in the Brexit Negotiations

Felix Steffek

1. Introduction

In this opinion piece, I argue that the Brexit negotiations need not be a zero or negative sum game, in which one side engages in claiming value to the detriment of the other. Instead, the negotiations can yield value if the parties remember where value is created: not at the level of the state, but at the level of the individuals affected. Therefore, the negotiators should embrace the challenge to create a new legal framework that benefits the interests of the individuals concerned, whether they live in the United Kingdom ('UK') or the European Union ('EU'). Where these interests differ, optional rules provide a way forward. Such optional rules would benefit those interested and would not create relevant negative consequences for those who are not. In addition, this new UK–EU framework could be the nucleus for a future success story. Once established, further countries could join – for example, those that are currently linked to the EU by association agreements.

2. Value Grabbing in Zero or Negative Sum Negotiations

A brief look at the news on any given day reveals that both the UK and the EU are involved in claiming value in a negotiation they consider to yield no value, or to even destroy value in aggregate. A recent instance is the disagreement on who has to pay how much in the 'Brexit bill'. On 22 May 2017, the EU governments renewed their pledge not to open negotiations about a post-Brexit framework before the UK promises to settle its debt with the EU.[1] Just one day before, Theresa May indicated that the EU had to settle its own debt for the UK's share in valuable assets, such as the European Investment Bank.[2] Relevant leading figures seem to believe that what lies ahead is even worse than grabbing as much of the cake as possible during the separation talks and shipping it back home. Comments such as the following from Donald Tusk, the President of the European Council, suggest that this is a negative sum negotiation: 'The brutal truth is that Brexit will be a loss for

---

[1] Alastair Macdonald, 'Failure Not Our Option, EU Says as Brexit Plan Set' (2017) <https://uk.reuters.com/article/uk-britain-eu-negotiations-idUKKBN18I1BJ> accessed 22 May 2017.

[2] Theresa May, 'Exclusive Interview with The Sunday Telegraph' (2017) <http://www.telegraph.co.uk/news/2017/05/20/theresa-may-exclusive-interview-not-abandoning-thatcherism/> accessed 22 May 2017.

all of us. There will be no cakes on the table. For anyone. There will be only salt and vinegar.'[3]

3. Value and Brexit

Before going into the details of value creation in the Brexit negotiations, the parties need to assure themselves what value means for their constituencies. Here, political philosophy – which is much in line with everyday perception – can contribute. Political philosophers of the modern age disagree about many things, but almost all of them share the opinion that governments and parliaments should act in the interests of all those individuals who are affected by their decisions. If the UK were to send Jeremy Bentham to the negotiating table and the EU would send Jean-Jacques Rousseau, they would agree that what they should seek to achieve is the best outcome for all individuals in their respective countries. Bentham, using his words, would strive for the 'greatest happiness of the greatest number'.[4] Rousseau would negotiate against the background that the General Will, as the foundation of the state, is based on the consent of the individuals.[5] Hence, the UK negotiators create value by fulfilling the interests of everyone affected by Brexit in the UK: those voting for and those voting against Brexit; those living in the UK, but not voting or not being entitled to vote; those calling themselves English, Welsh, Scottish or Northern Irish; and those coming from the EU or the wider world but living in the UK. Combining the two key sentences of Theresa May's premiership leads the way. If 'Brexit means Brexit',[6] and if the aim is to make the UK 'a country that works for everyone',[7] then 'Brexit means Brexit that works for everyone'. Vice versa, the same is true for the remaining EU Member States. Good Brexit negotiations are in the interests of everyone affected in the other EU 27 countries, and that includes UK citizens living in other EU countries.

4. How to Create Value for Those Affected by Brexit?

At first sight, developing strategies for positive-sum Brexit negotiations may seem a daunting task. This is not, however, because it is any more difficult than devising value distributing strategies in a negative sum game. Rather, it

---

[3] Donald Tusk, 'Speech by President Donald Tusk at the European Policy Centre Conference (Speech 575/16)' (European Policy Centre Conference, 13 October 2016) <http://www.consilium.europa.eu/en/press/press-releases/2016/10/13-tusk-speech-epc/> accessed 5 June 2017.

[4] Jeremy Bentham, *A Fragment on Government* (London 1776) ii (Preface).

[5] Jean-Jacques Rousseau, *Du Contrat Social* (Amsterdam 1762) 16 ff.

[6] Theresa May, 'Speech' (Conservative Party Conference, Birmingham, 2 October 2016) < https://www.politicshome.com/news/uk/political-parties/conservative-party/news/79517/read-full-theresa-mays-conservative> accessed 5 June 2017.

[7] Theresa May, 'Speech' (Conservative Party Conference, Birmingham, 5 October 2016) < http://www.independent.co.uk/news/uk/politics/theresa-may-speech-tory-conference-2016-in-full-transcript-a7346171.html> accessed 5 June 2017.

is because hardly any of the lead negotiators has really started thinking and talking about creating value. Here is an invitation to follow a quick sketch of just one example for creating value in the negotiations. It rests on the insight that value creation is not about the position of the 28 Member States before and after the conclusion of the negotiations, but about the interests of the individuals in the Member States affected. Brexit is not about states, it is about those represented by states. The logic of this is to create a shared legal framework the people in the UK and the EU may opt into. This UK–EU framework operates under two conditions: (1) no-one who does not opt in is disproportionately affected in a negative way; (2) where either the UK or the EU believes that such opt-in comes at a cost for them, they will negotiate a price that those opting in will pay. The point is that opt-ins and prices are decided and paid at the level of the individuals, not at the level of the states.

Here is an example taken from company law. Let the founders of companies decide whether to opt into a UK–EU company law that is administered by a register and court system overseen by a new body established in the Brexit contract. As company law predominantly concerns the internal relationships of the company, those not opting in would not be affected negatively – at least not disproportionately. If the UK or the EU thinks that such a regime creates costs, these costs could be charged to the founders. Let them decide whether or not the rules opted into are worth the costs. The starting point for such a regime could be the EU company law already established. This seems to be acceptable, since the UK already signalled that it would accept EU law currently implemented in its legal system. These rules could certainly be developed and amended thereafter. This also seems to be a feasible approach since, once the necessary court and register are established, it would suffice to have a schedule to the Brexit contract listing all current EU instruments that are dealt with in this way. Another strong candidate is the European Insolvency Regulation ('EIR'), in which the EU and the UK both have an interest. In particular, the UK actively opted into the application of the EIR, showing that there is value seen in a common framework. Modern developments in information technology, such as smart contracts, facilitate such an 'individual approach' to law-making.

5. Common values for the UK and EU post-Brexit

The new framework briefly sketched above promises a chance for value creation for both the UK and the EU beyond the mere Brexit theme. The new UK–EU international scheme could be opened to other countries with which closer ties are desirable. Currently, there are 23 EU association agreements in force – for example, with Georgia, Iceland, Norway, and South Africa. Further association agreements are under negotiation or ratification – for example, with San Marino and the Ukraine. Some of those countries could join the scheme and their interest would be a success story for the UK and the EU as a nucleus team. In fact, it would offer both the UK and the EU a common project after Brexit. In addition, the legal framework and opt-in possibilities could be extended after the deal is closed within the two-year negotiation period. It would not be a failure if, in the beginning, only some areas would be taken under the umbrella of the scheme. Others could easily be added later. In any case, adapting a well-known dictum of the legendary soccer coach S. Herberger ('After the game is before the game'), with Brexit, after the negotiations is before the negotiations.

6. Conclusion

The core message is to move the focus from the position of the Member States before and after the UK leaves the EU towards the interests of the individuals affected by this event. Establishing a framework of choice at the level of the individuals affected is one example of a strategy promising value creation in the Brexit talks. This should also appeal to the political strategists in the negotiation teams. Instead of negotiating one solution for electorates with divided opinions, the negotiators could offer attractive rules for all concerned. The approach suggested would work even if the UK or the EU were to consider areas such as immigration or sovereignty to be off-limits. There are many more examples for an option approach than those sketched here. In any case, this is the discussion that should start now and replace the fight over a cake that might turn out to taste like vinegar.

Felix Steffek is a University Lecturer at the Faculty
of Law of the University of Cambridge
and a Senior Member of Newnham College.

Brexit Negotiations – Process Proposals

Andreas Hacke

With the Article 50-notification put on the table in Brussels on 29 March 2017, Theresa May has formally started the Brexit negotiations' process. There is a lot at stake for all parties concerned. What has been aired so far from both sides of the table in preparation of the talks (eg, the drawing of 'red lines' such as the link between access to the single market and free movement of people, the European Union's ('EU's) 'Brexit bill' of 60 billion Euro, the idea of 'punishing' the United Kingdom ('UK') for its decision to leave, the 'use' of EU nationals resident in the UK as a bargaining chip, the signalling of a possible race to the bottom with respect to tax rates, etc) looks very much like classical positional bargaining with a clear focus on value claiming. The negotiations are thereby in danger to get stuck amid the negotiators' dilemma and to turn into a lose-lose game.[1]

As Horst Eidenmüller and I have recently proposed,[2] negotiations can be understood as a structure of three levels: problem, people, and process. Engaging in positional bargaining tactics (instead of focussing on interests) and focussing on claiming value (instead of on creating value) at the *problem level* often materializes in aggressive communication and negative emotions at the *people level*. This, in turn, lets the negotiation *process* often run into deadlocks and be far less smooth and constructive than would be possible. By contrast, a structured and actively managed negotiation *process* can have positive repercussions both on the *people* and, thereby, also on the *problem* level. Process design and management thus lie at the heart of negotiation management. Process is key.

What can negotiation process design contribute to the Brexit negotiations with a view to re-focus on the interests of all parties concerned and to safeguard as much value creation (or at least protection) as possible, so that the game may be changed into a winning game (or at least into a lose less game) for everyone? There are at least four aspects of process design to consider:[3]

---

[1] David Lax and James Sebenius, 'The Manager as Negotiator: The Negotiator's Dilemma: Creating and Claiming Value' in Goldberg, Sander and Rogers (eds) *Dispute Resolution* (2nd edn, 1992) 49–62.

[2] Horst Eidenmüller and Andreas Hacke, 'The PPP Negotiation Model: Problem, People, and Process' (*Oxford Business Law Blog*, 17 March 2017) <https://www.law.ox.ac.uk/business-law-blog/blog/2017/03/ppp-negotiation-model-problem-people-and-process> accessed 6 June 2017.

[3] For aspects of process design, see also David Lax and James Sebenius, '3D Negotiation: Powerful Tools to Change the Game in Your Most Important Deals' (1st edn, Harvard Business School Press 2006).

1. Who?

First, process design should take into account who will be leading the negotiations.[4] While the UK will be represented by its government, notably by Prime Minister Theresa May and by Brexit secretary David Davis, things are more complicated on the EU side: the EU Treaties vest the European Council (ie, the heads of the Member States) with the ultimate negotiation power. It is the European Council who shall issue the EU's negotiation guidelines, who shall nominate the 'Union negotiator' and who has the authority – subject to consent by the European Parliament – to finally conclude any Brexit deal on behalf of the EU (Art 50(2) Treaty on European Union ('TEU') in conjunction with Art 218(3) Treaty on the Functioning of the European Union ('TFEU')).

That said, the European Council has chosen the European Commission (the 'Commission') as the EU lead negotiator, which, in turn, has delegated this task to former commissioner Michel Barnier. Mr Barnier has installed a small 'Article 50 task force'[5] whose members will be leading and coordinating the talks on the side of the EU. This setup poses the risk of a classical 'principal-agent-dilemma'. On the one hand, the Commission (the 'agent') has, of course, its own interests in the upcoming negotiations, partially distinct from those of the Member States (the 'principals'). On the other hand, it will ultimately not be the Commission (nor Mr Barnier) who will strike or block any deal, but the European Council.

The Process should therefore be designed so as to avoid the typical principal-agent-trap of talking to the agent who – at the end of lengthy discussions – hides behind his principal (who then uses his or her leverage and time pressure to push through further demands). Thus, the UK should strive to keep very close ties with the EU Member States' governments in parallel to continuing the talks with the Commission's task force to assure that what is being said at the negotiation table is also ultimately backed by the principal. The same holds true *vice versa*: it should also be in the interest of the Member States to very closely monitor the work of Mr Barnier and his task force to make sure that the deal they are preparing is also a workable deal for the Member States.

Turning back to the UK, it would arguably be strategically better for Theresa May to also delegate the talks to someone more remote from the government than herself or even her Brexit secretary (eg, some 'elder statesman'), in order to also benefit from the advantages that agency relationships have for the

---

[4] Christian Bühring-Uhle, Horst Eidenmüller and Andreas Nelle, *Verhandlungsmanagement* (2nd edn, Beck im dtv 2017) 173 ff.

[5] European Commission, 'Taskforce on Article 50 negotiations with the United Kingdom' <https://ec.europa.eu/info/departments/taskforce-article-50-negotiations-united-kingdom_en> accessed 6 June 2017.

principal, notably a higher degree of flexibility and leeway. From a negotiation management perspective, it is thus surprising that Theresa May has – quite to the contrary – apparently restated her intention to lead the talks herself in her famous dinner with Jean-Claude Juncker at Downing Street 10.[6]

2. When?

A second important factor of process design is timing. Much has been said and written about the two-year deadline of Art. 50(3) TEU, at the end of which, and in the absence of any deal signed by then, the UK will automatically exit the EU ('Hardest Brexit'). Given the (upcoming) general elections both in the UK and in Germany, the necessary ratification process on the side of the UK, the need for consent by the European Parliament and a 'super qualified majority' within the European Council (Art 50(4) TEU and Art 238(3)(b) TFEU), the real time-frame will be much shorter – less than 18 months according to Mr Barnier.

It is obvious that this is too short a time to reach detailed agreements on all issues that need to be resolved. Therefore, process design might consider mechanisms to alleviate these time constraints. There are at least two possible ways to achieve this: first, Art 50(3) TEU itself allows for an extension of the negotiation period by unanimous decision of the European Council in agreement with the UK. As demanding as this might seem politically: considering the joint interest of the parties in a structured and promising process, they should at least contemplate using this mechanism to allow themselves more time; the second possibility is implicated by the stipulation in Art 50(3) TEU that 'the Treaties shall cease to apply to the State in question *from the date of entry into force of the withdrawal agreement....*'. The parties could therefore conclude any form of generic withdrawal agreement within the two-year timeframe and agree therein to suspend its *entry into force* until other prerequisites are met thereafter (eg, until a more detailed agreement on the future relationship is reached, or simply until an additional time period has elapsed). By this token, the parties would automatically create a transition period in which the process of the UK leaving the EU in legal terms could be orderly managed and happen less sharply.

3. What?

Third, and closely linked to the timing issue, process design should address the order in which distinct steps in the negotiation process are taken: if it is true that mere positional bargaining can have the parties lose sight of their

---

[6] Thomas Gutschker, 'Das desaströse Brexit-Dinner' *Frankfurter Allgemeine Sonntagszeitung* (Frankfurt, 1 May 2017) <http://www.faz.net/aktuell/brexit/juncker-bei-may-das-desastroese-brexit-dinner-14993605.html> accessed 26 May 2017.

interests and stifle value creation moves,[7] a procedure in which positional bargaining comes last should be agreed upon.

Therefore, instead of haggling over the mere positional question of whether to first discuss the divorce and then the terms of the future relationship (as the EU wishes) or to do both in parallel (as the UK intends), the parties should agree on a joint 'roadmap' for their talks, structuring them in three distinct phases. In a first phase, they should outline their respective interests as guidelines for all further bargains. To that aim, they should first collect and then prioritize all interests under discussion, eg by using a joint scoring system. This should encompass the interests of all stakeholders concerned: those of the UK (and its citizens), those of the EU as an institution, and those of the Member States (and their citizens). On that basis, the parties should dedicate a second phase specifically to value creation. In this phase, they should brainstorm on sources for mutual gain and on areas of possible common losses ('lose-only items'). Only then should the parties – in a third and last phase – engage in real bargaining over single issues and, thus, in claiming value with the aim of reaching an agreement. By following such a structured approach, following an agreed joint roadmap, the process could be designed to limit the negative effects of positional bargaining and to safeguard as much interest focus and value creation as possible.

4. How?

Fourth, and finally, the parties should agree on the continued joint management of the process. To that end, they could install, at the very outset, a joint process management and moderating facility (a 'process steering committee'), which would exclusively focus on the process as such. This facility would keep an eye on the progress made, evaluate whether the process lives up to the promise of its original design, and – if not – make proposals as to how to amend the process to factor in any intermediate developments. Further, such facility could monitor whether all procedural steps and rules as agreed between the parties are being observed, thus fulfilling a 'housekeeping' role.

It is obvious that, against the background of their potentially conflicting interests, the unilateral or joint management of the procedural tasks proposed herein poses significant additional challenges for the parties. This might be a reason why the parties should consider bringing in neutral third parties to assist the negotiations as mediators.[8] In any case, the multiple issues at stake

---

[7] For the dichotomy between interests and positions see Roger Fisher, William Ury and Bruce Patton, *Getting to Yes: Negotiating Agreement Without Giving In* (3rd edn, London: Penguin 2012) 4 ff, 40 ff.

[8] See Horst Eidenmüller 'Negotiating and Mediating Brexit' (*Oxford Business Law Blog*, 23 December 2016) <https://www.law.ox.ac.uk/business-law-blog/blog/2016/12/negotiating-and-mediating-brexit> accessed 26 May 2017; Horst Eidenmüller, 'Negotiating and Mediating Brexit' (2016) Pepp L Rev 39; more generally on the method of mediation, Christian Duve, Horst Eidenmüller and Andreas Hacke, *Mediation in der Wirtschaft* (2nd edn, Cologne: Otto Schmidt 2011).

in the upcoming Brexit negotiations will be even more at risk in a poorly designed and managed process. Therefore, the parties must take responsibility not only for the *problems* they discuss, but also for the *process* which they use to discuss them.

Andreas Hacke is partner at the law firm
Zwanzig Hacke Meilke & Partner
and a Visiting Lecturer at the University of Oxford.

How To Negotiate A Successful Brexit

Horst Eidenmüller

Prime Minister Theresa May has promised to make Brexit a success. This will be difficult: the European Union ('EU') has brought the United Kingdom ('UK') significant economic benefits and prosperity. How can the UK be better off with Brexit? Everything depends on which factors are part of the equation and how they are ranked – Brexit will of course enhance the UK's political autonomy. But much more is at stake: security, the stability of the UK, (distributive) justice ('A Country That Works For Everyone'[1]), etc. How precisely shall we assess success or failure?

Even if the goal were clear, the road to a successful Brexit is unknown. Quite possibly, no such road exists. Literally thousands of negotiations with a multiplicity of counterparties will have to be conducted. Most important will be the negotiations on a withdrawal agreement with the EU in accordance with Article 50 of the Treaty on the Functioning of the European Union ('TFEU'). How shall all these negotiations be approached? What might be a successful negotiation strategy?

In this short article, I discuss a couple of guideposts for those who are charged with negotiating (a successful) Brexit. I derive these from applied game and negotiation theory,[2] my own experience as a negotiator and mediator and (casual) observations of the first moves and developments in the 'Brexit Negotiation Games'[3] since the referendum in 2016.

1. Focus on interests instead of positions

In her speech at Lancaster House on 17 January 2017, Theresa May laid out her plan for a 'Global Britain'.[4] In this speech, the phrase 'I want...' figures prominently: it is repeated 12 times. In the jargon of negotiation theory, Mrs May talked a lot about positions (and demands), much less about interests.

---

[1] See Theresa May, 'Speech' (Tory Party Conference, Birmingham, 5 October 2016) <https://www.youtube.com/watch?v=Bmw7blQp8XY> accessed 20 May 2017.

[2] The literature is of course vast. See, for example, Avinash Dixit and Barry J Nalebuff, *The Art of Strategy* (NY: Norton 2008); Roger Fisher, William Ury and Bruce Patton, *Getting to Yes: Negotiating Agreement Without Giving In* (3rd edn, London: Penguin 2011); Deepak Malhotra and Max Bazerman, *Negotiation Genius* (NY: Bantam 2007); Deepak Malhotra, *Negotiating the Impossible* (Oakland: Berrett-Koehler 2016); Christian Bühring-Uhle, Horst Eidenmüller and Andreas Nelle, *Verhandlungsmanagement* (2nd edn, München: Beck 2017).

[3] See Horst Eidenmüller, 'Brexit Negotiation Games' [2006] OBLB <https://www.law.ox.-ac.uk/business-law-blog/blog/2016/06/brexit-negotiation-games> accessed 20 May 2017.

[4] See Theresa May, 'A Global Britain' (2017) <https://images.derstandard.at/2017/01/17/170117-A-Global-Britain-FINAL.pdf> accessed 20 May 2017.

However, interests are key. They motivate or drive bargaining positions. Often, an interest can be satisfied by very different positions. For example, compensation for harm can come in the form of money, goods or gifts, and/ or an apology. This opens up the potential for value creation – or at least preservation – in negotiations: instead of compromising positions, you are looking for deals or deal elements that (best) satisfy interests.

To do this well, interests must be ranked or prioritised: each side 'compromises' less highly-valued interests to obtain something with respect to more highly-valued interests in return ('logrolling'). Sophisticated negotiators prepare for negotiations by using scoring-systems to map the 'interest landscape', including priorities. A clear focus on interests also shows in your communication style. Instead of 'I want…', you (should) say 'It is (very) important for us…' or 'We (urgently) need…', etc.

2. Put yourself in their shoes

It takes two to tango: to get a good or even excellent deal, something must be put on the table that is good or even excellent for the other side as well. To do this (well), you have to think hard about their interests and priorities: What do they need? How important is this to them, and why?

Good negotiators put themselves into the shoes of their negotiation partner by, for example, engaging in role reversal exercises when preparing for a negotiation, or by asking good (open-ended) questions when negotiating, and by listening actively. They think hard about deal-sweeteners for the other side and build them a golden bridge to saying yes. They might even help write the victory speech of their opponent.[5]

Theresa May's Lancaster House speech is not only replete with bargaining positions. It is also full of what she wants or hopes to get (for Britain): 'I want…', 'I will…'. Of course, this was primarily a political speech directed towards a domestic audience, calibrated to demonstrate leadership. However, when it comes to striking a bargain with Mr Barnier, Mrs May and her aides will be well advised to think hard about his (not her) political victory speech (and that of Mr Macron and Mrs Merkel).

I should add that this principle of course also applies to the EU side in the Brexit negotiations. To build the UK a golden bridge to *stay* in the EU – which, I submit, is in the interest of all Member States –, something in the institutional setup of the EU could and would need to be changed. Dissatisfaction with the bureaucracy in Brussels is not limited to the UK. Giving back power and control to the Member States and (somewhat) disempowering the EU Commission could be a step in this direction.

---

[5] See William Ury, *Getting Past No: Negotiating Your Way from Confrontation to Cooperation* (NY: Bantam Books 1993).

3. Look out for ways to create value

Real-life negotiations are about creating and claiming value – they are usually positive-sum rather than zero-sum or even negative-sum games. Even the Brexit negotiations hold the potential for value creation, or at least value preservation. However, they have been approached by all parties so far as if they were purely distributive in nature: red lines have been drawn (eg, no cherry-picking with respect to the fundamental freedoms, no jurisdiction of the European Court of Justice), and threats have been issued (eg, the UK as a tax heaven, less cooperation on security issues if there is no trade deal).

It pays to think hard about potential value-creating moves. As in many commercial negotiations, the key to finding such moves often lies in (little) differences between the parties: differences with respect to interests, forecasts, risk attitudes, capabilities, etc. If parties entertain different views as to future contingencies, contingent contracts that build on these contingencies can be drawn in ways that create value. Might it be possible, for example, to tie the UK's Brexit bill to contingencies such as currency exchange rates, Gross Domestic Product ('GDP') developments in the UK or the Eurozone, etc?

4. Make small trust-enhancing moves

When thinking about what to do, negotiators often find themselves in a dilemma that is similarly structured to the famous prisoners' dilemma: the negotiators' dilemma.[6] It appears to be a dominant strategy to claim value – either to protect yourself against being exploited or to exploit the other side. Hence, all parties apply value-claiming tactics, missing opportunities for value creation.

As with the prisoners' dilemma, a tested way out of the dilemma is playing 'tit for tat': start out with a small cooperative move – don't risk too much –, and then mirror the tactic of your opponent in all subsequent negotiating rounds.[7] By starting out cooperatively, you build trust and signal your readiness to bargain for a mutually beneficial outcome. You don't stand to lose much if you anticipate that there is a high likelihood that your move will be reciprocated.

An excellent opportunity to make a small trust-enhancing move exists with respect to the residency status of (continental) Europeans living and working in the UK and Britons living and working in (continental) Europe. It seems highly likely that, eventually, reciprocal residency rights will be agreed upon in the negotiations. If so, why does one side not move in this direction right now? Trust and political goodwill could and would be created. Unfortunately,

---

[6] See David Lax and James Sebenius, *The Manager as Negotiator: Bargaining for Coopera-tion and Competitive Gain* (NY and London: The Free Press, 1986).

[7] See Robert Axelrod, *The Evolution of Cooperation* (NY: Basic Books 1984).

neither side has seized this opportunity so far, instead using people as bargaining chips – neither very smart, nor very human. The UK still has a lot to gain by doing the right thing *first*.

5. Improve (the perception of) your 'BATNA'

Whether Brexit can be made a success of course not only depends on how much value can be created at the bargaining table; it also depends on what will happen if the negotiations on a withdrawal agreement fail, ie if there is a 'Sharp Brexit'. The quality of the UK's 'Best Alternative to a Negotiated Agreement' ('BATNA') relative to that of the EU determines what kind of deal the UK will be able to negotiate. More specifically, it is the *perception* of this quality by the respective other side that is crucial.[8]

Hence, it was an effective move to claim value when the House of Lords European Union Committee concluded in its report of 4 March 2017 that '…if agreement is not reached,…the UK would be subject to no enforceable obligation to make any financial contribution [to the EU budget] at all.'[9] It was much less effective when Theresa May threatened in her 29 March 2017 withdrawal letter[10] that '[i]n security terms a failure to reach agreement would mean our cooperation in the fight against crime and terrorism would be weakened.' While the UK can credibly threaten to litigate the issue of a potential Brexit bill and its size, weakening cooperation in the fight against crime and terrorism is not in the UK's self-interest. Hence, this is an empty threat.

Further, the UK can and should emphasise that trading on World Trade Organisation ('WTO') terms – if the negotiations on a withdrawal agreement fail – would not be in the interest of other key Member States such as Germany with its significant levels of exports. Germany has a crucial interest in negotiating a 'new deep and special partnership' as envisaged by Mrs May – possibly by making disproportionately large(r) contributions to the EU budget in return for a 'special' access to the UK market.

6. Be attentive to process issues

Any negotiation is a *process* in which *people* try to resolve a *problem*.[11] These are three different layers, and whatever happens in a negotiation happens on

---

[8] See Bühring-Uhle/Eidenmüller/Nelle (n2).

[9] See House of Lords European Union Committee, 'Brexit and the EU budget' (2017) <https://www.publications.parliament.uk/pa/ld201617/ldselect/ldeucom/125/125.pdf> accessed 21 May 2017.

[10] For the full text of the letter see, for example, Reuters, 'Text of PM May's letter to EU's Tusk triggering Brexit process' (2017) <http://uk.reuters.com/article/uk-britain-eu-letter-text-idUKKBN1701JH> accessed 21 May 2017.

[11] See Horst Eidenmüller and Andreas Hacke, 'The PPP Negotiation Model: Problem, People, and Process' (2017) OBLB <https://www.law.ox.ac.uk/business-law-blog/blog/2017/03/ppp-negotiation-model-problem-people-and-process> accessed 21 May 2017.

one or more of these layers. Earlier approaches to negotiation management focused on the problem and the people layers of negotiations, and neglected the process layer. That was a significant deficiency. Proactively designing an efficient negotiation process can be most conducive to building a good people relationship and to amicably solving difficult negotiation problems. Conversely, a disorganised process will make it unlikely that negotiations concerning the problem move forward constructively, or that the negotiators are able to establish good rapport with each other.

Both analytically and in communications, negotiators should keep these three layers separate. Hence, it was unfortunate that the UK's Article 50 notification letter mixed everything together: a legal declaration, process proposals, bargaining positions, threats, interests, and plans for a 'deep and special partnership'.

When the negotiations start in June, the UK should suggest having a discussion about process – and only process – first: who shall negotiate with whom over what and when in the two years to come? Devising a comprehensive and detailed negotiation plan should be the key task for the first meetings.

A crucial issue here will be sequencing: the UK wishes to negotiate the terms of withdrawal alongside those of a new partnership, whereas the Union insists on settling the terms of Brexit first.[12] There are good reasons for the Union's position: it disentangles claiming value (Brexit bill) and creating value (new partnership), breaking up the negotiators' dilemma, and it corresponds to common sense – get a divorce before you remarry. Further, settling the Brexit bill might even allow for some value creation (see *supra* at 3), and the UK appears to have nothing to lose: the Union itself subscribes to the '…principle that nothing is agreed until everything is agreed…'.[13] On the other hand, even provisionally agreeing to a significant 'Brexit payment' or, conversely, significantly reducing prior demands may be extremely difficult to 'sell' politically – with the looming risk of deadlock right at the start of the negotiations. Hence, both sides have another opportunity to make a small trust-enhancing move – on the process level.

7. Think strategically

Negotiations are a form of strategic interaction: you devise and attempt to implement a plan; how well you do also depends on the plan and the moves

---

[12] For the EU approach, see European Council, 'European Council (Art 50) guidelines for Brexit negotiations' (2017) <http://www.consilium.europa.eu/en/press/press-releases/2017/04/29-euco-brexit-guidelines/> accessed 21 May 2017; Council of the European Union, 'Directives for the negotiation of an agreement with the United Kingdom of Great Britain and Northern Ireland setting out the arrangements for its withdrawal from the European Union' (2017) <http://www.consilium.europa.eu/en/press/press-releases/2017/05/22-brexit-negotiating-directives/> accessed 23 May 2017.

[13] *Ibid.*

of your negotiation partner. Strategic (inter)action takes place on the process level, such as with the sequencing issue just discussed. It also takes place at the problem level: binding commitments, for example, are a high-risk, but also potentially highly effective form of claiming value.[14]

As is obvious, the interests of the remaining Member States in the withdrawal negotiations are not homogenous. Is this a strategic weakness that could be exploited by the UK? The Union itself appears to think so: 'So as not to undercut the position of the Union, there will be no separate negotiations between individual Member States and the United Kingdom on matters pertaining to the withdrawal of the United Kingdom from the Union.'[15] However, while large Member States such as Germany and France acting together with Italy, Spain or Poland can *block* any withdrawal agreement in the Council, *passing* any such agreement requires the consent of 19 or more of the remaining Member States.[16]

Hence, there is probably little for the UK to gain by attempting to undercut the agency relationship between the Member States and the European Commission in the Brexit negotiations. Rather, the British government is well advised to take the mandate of the European Commission seriously and work with its 'Taskforce on Article 50 negotiations'[17] constructively – provided that the European Commission faithfully acts as the agent of the Member States and does not pursue a hidden agenda of fostering its own interests.

The UK's negotiators will face challenging strategic issues in particular with respect to the trade deals with third countries that it needs to negotiate. If the EU has a trade deal in place, the easiest 'solution' is probably to maintain this agreement for the UK after Brexit. While this might be the legal outcome in some cases anyway – depending on intricate questions of public international law and the precise wording of the agreement –, legal certainty will be fostered if affected parties confirm this position. Where no agreements exist, the UK will probably attempt to focus first on the partners that are the most important (in trade terms) and promise a fast and, hopefully, attractive deal that establishes a reference point for future negotiations. This may prove difficult as many countries will want to know the outcome of EU-UK talks before making their own commitments.[18]

---

[14] See Thomas Schelling, *The Strategy of Conflict* (Cambridge, MA: Harvard University Press, 1960).

[15] *Ibid* (n12).

[16] See Eidenmüller (n3).

[17] See European Commission 'Taskforce on Article 50 negotiations with the United Kingdom' <https://ec.europa.eu/info/departments/taskforce-article-50-negotiations-united-kingdom_en> accessed 21 May 2017.

[18] See Paul McLean, 'Let the haggling begin', FT of 31 May 2017, p. 7.

8. Consider mediation

Brexit will be implemented by thousands of extremely complex negotiations: these involve a multiplicity of parties with heterogeneous interests and multiple difficult issues and problems. The challenges for an effective process management are enormous. No neutral third party is involved so far. To date, the negotiation dynamic has been characterised by positional bargaining and value-claiming. The risk of a lose/lose outcome is real and severe. At the same time, the potential for creating or at least preserving value exists as well.

In this situation, especially highly skilled negotiators would consider mediation.[19] Experience tells us that creating or at least preserving value in extremely complex multi-party negotiations will be much more likely if mediators guide the parties' negotiations. This holds true for purely commercial negotiations, as well as for negotiations with a (strong) political or public element.

Brexit can be mediated. A potential 'Brexit Mediation Model' could involve monthly 'High-Level Talks', mediated by a team of three mediators (from the UK, the EU, and a third country) and geared towards identifying and agreeing upon the key elements of a withdrawal agreement, a transition agreement, and the principles underlying the new relationship between the EU and the UK.

Brexit might not be mediated: overconfidence of the parties and negotiators, an underestimation of the benefits of mediation, or fear of lack of control, for example, might prevent the use of mediation to resolve Brexit. As all seasoned dispute resolution practitioners know, these obstacles can be overcome. In the interest of the UK, the future of Europe, and indeed, the world as a whole, Brexit should be mediated – now.

Horst Eidenmüller is the Freshfields Professor
of Commercial Law at the University of Oxford.

---

[19] See Horst Eidenmüller, 'Negotiating and Mediating Brexit' (2016) Pepp L Rev 39.

Index